Every informed and active parent [will] want to read *Reclaiming Education* [...] the most acclaimed learning specia[lists in] the country, helps you navigate the school years with finesse and confidence.

DRS. LES & LESLIE PARROTT, *New York Times* bestselling authors of *Saving Your Marriage Before It Starts*

The greatest trick the devil played was to convince us he didn't exist, and the singular trick government schools managed was to convince us they weren't religious. Every school is a religious school, and Christian families would do well to read Cynthia Tobias's book *Reclaiming Education* to better understand how to raise their children in the fear and admonition of the Lord, not government.

SAM SORBO, producer at Sorbo Studios and author of *They're Your Kids*

In her new book, *Reclaiming Education*, my friend and child-learning specialist Cynthia Tobias has compiled an immensely practical and commonsense approach to understanding the various learning styles of children and how to tailor their education around those styles for maximum learning experiences—whether in public school, homeschool, or private school. She also deftly illustrates the Trojan horses of modern public education to indoctrinate our children with values we dislike—and what to do about it! Cynthia sounds the alarm and calls us to be diligent in, knowledgeable about, and involved with our children's education. Parents, get this book and get educated yourself on how best to teach your kids! They deserve it.

JOE BATTAGLIA, president of Renaissance Communications, broadcaster, and author of *The Politically Incorrect Jesus* and *Unfriended*

I strongly recommend *Reclaiming Education* for all parents and teachers. It's a quick, compelling read, and the workbook puts practical tools and strategies right in kids' hands. I use the downloadable student workbooks with my middle-school classes at my Christian school, and they love finding out how their natural strengths can help them be more successful in *all* their classes. It's really made a difference, especially when we have kids who are smart and capable but struggle with standard methods of learning.

KELLI SOYRING, teacher at Sound Christian Academy in Tacoma, Washington; voted Teacher of the Year by *South Sound Magazine* in 2022

Reclaiming Education

TEACH YOUR CHILD
TO BE A CONFIDENT LEARNER

Cynthia Ulrich Tobias

with Mary Jo Dean

FOCUS
ON
THE FAMILY.

A Focus on the Family resource
published by Tyndale House Publishers

Contents

To my husband, Jack Talley, who provided endless support and encouragement; and my sister, Sandee Baker, who was always ready to cheerfully proofread and give me valuable feedback.

CYNTHIA

To my husband, Brennan; thank you for your love and support. I love you.

To Spencer, Sawyer, and Annie; thank you for your grace, patience, and perseverance. You have made my life so incredibly wonderful. I'll love you forever . . . you know the rest.

MARY JO

Foreword

OUR TEAM AT Focus on the Family considers it a privilege to partner with Cynthia Tobias in publishing her latest book, *Reclaiming Education*. I've had the honor of knowing Cynthia personally for many years now. She is an experienced, extraordinary educator with a genuine heart to help children learn best . . . in the *ways* they learn best. Not only does she want to equip parents to raise educated children, but she also wants to see those children become adults who love the Lord and continue learning joyfully, and to His glory, for the rest of their days.

This volume is aptly named. Never has it been more crucial for parents to "reclaim education"—in other words, to take a close look at the state of education in our country so they can wisely and prayerfully weigh their choices and, ultimately, provide the best academic approach and setting for their children. I'm well aware that there are many dedicated teachers and school administrators serving tirelessly in our educational system. However, we must also acknowledge the ideological battlefield that public education has become. Teachers' unions and other political forces have arrayed themselves against parents and are doing everything possible to indoctrinate children into social beliefs that lie far outside the mainstream, traditional understanding of education.

I will go so far as to say that, if my sons were starting elementary school today, I would not enroll them in a public school. I certainly realize that each parent has complex and unique circumstances that must be considered. Nonetheless, if you are staring an educational decision in the face, I would simply urge you to think and pray carefully about whether you will introduce your children to a system that becomes more intellectually, morally, and spiritually bankrupt with every passing day.

Throughout this book, Cynthia offers invaluable insight and encouragement about the various learning styles and how they can be harnessed to optimize a child's academic success without compromising his or her character. I don't know anyone more knowledgeable about what makes children tick, and Cynthia's practical tips are sure to be helpful regardless of your own children's individual learning styles or personality bents.

Meanwhile, Cynthia's coauthor, Mary Jo Dean, challenges you to leave the homeschooling option on the table! Millions of families around the country have embraced this lifestyle as a means of instilling biblical faith and traditional values in their children, inspiring a lifelong passion for learning, discovering their unique gifts and callings, and resisting the culture's relentless efforts to pull them away from their Christian upbringing. By and large, homeschooled children are thoughtful, mature, and well-adjusted, and I believe that's because their primary influencers are their parents.

If the thought of stepping outside the educational box seems overwhelming, take heart! Within these pages, you will discover that you can escape the bonds of a one-size-fits-all educational model and find how to maximize your children's learning potential. What's more, when you discover the environment and tools that best dovetail with their distinct, God-given strengths and weaknesses, you will set them on a path toward learning that will continue long after the diplomas are handed out.

Jim Daly
President, Focus on the Family

Preface

Your Child *Can* Succeed

WAR HAS BEEN DECLARED on the families of America. What's at stake? The hearts and minds of our children. Who is the enemy? Those who would replace education with indoctrination. Those who would insist that parents step back and let federal and state organizations and teachers' unions legislate the content and direction of what students will learn and how they will learn it.

But you as a parent are the first line of defense in this battle. God has entrusted your children to you, and you're designed to love and protect them more than anyone else can. You are their first and most influential teacher, and your home is their first classroom. You know them better than anyone.

When it's time to begin their formal schooling, how you choose to educate your children matters more than you can possibly imagine. Public, private, charter school, homeschool, or a combination of any or all of these—you can't afford to base your decisions strictly on convenience or finances.

We parents need to take an active role in equipping our children to succeed in school and beyond. In a world that pressures them at every turn to simply conform to and comply with a secular worldview, we need to weave a strong and enduring commitment to God into the very fabric of their lives. We need to make sure they know they have been fearfully and wonderfully made by their creator and designer.

This book will show how public education is failing our children, and the latter part will speak to workable alternatives, including homeschooling. But however you decide to educate your children, this book will equip you to teach them how to succeed as lifelong learners in *any* academic setting. That doesn't mean simply making learning easier for them. It certainly doesn't mean lowering any standards or compromising on discipline and behavior. It means teaching each child to discover his or her natural, inborn strengths and figure out ways to use them in order to learn. Accountability stays intact. The important thing is to use their *strengths*—we can't build on weakness. And the world needs their kinds of strengths more than ever.

Our fervent prayer is that you will read this book with an open mind and heart. We pray you will take the time to truly help your children recognize and understand how their minds are wired for taking in and processing information and how they can motivate themselves to learn, even in the most challenging and difficult of circumstances.

Every child you have is God's gift to you. It's not a coincidence that you got the kids you've got. God chose you to nurture and guide your children to adulthood. And we don't believe it's a coincidence that you're reading this book. We can't wait to see what God will do.

PART ONE

Why You Need to Reclaim Your Child's Education

1

Problem:
Public Schools Are Failing

Write these commandments that I've given you today on your hearts. Get them inside of you and then get them inside your children. Talk about them wherever you are, sitting at home or walking in the street; talk about them from the time you get up in the morning to when you fall into bed at night. Tie them on your hands and foreheads as a reminder; inscribe them on the doorposts of your homes and on your city gates.

DEUTERONOMY 6:6-9 (MSG)

SEVERAL YEARS AGO, I (Cynthia) was speaking on base for a group of Air Force wives, and I used Proverbs 22:6 as my text: "Train up a child in the way he should go, and when he is old he will not depart from it" (NKJV).

I then pointed out how the Amplified version of the Bible goes into more detail: "Train up a child in the way he should go [and in keeping with his individual gift or bent], and when he is old he will not depart from it" (AMPC).

We spent the next ninety minutes talking about how important it is to understand that no two children are alike and exploring the many different ways we could bring out the best in each child.

3

After my presentation, the Air Force chaplain stepped up to talk to me. He explained that he had spent many years studying the original Greek and Hebrew used in the Bible. He said, "I appreciate your emphasis on getting to know every child's strengths. I want to give you an insight that illustrates how critical that concept actually is."

He went on to explain that in Proverbs 22:6, the Hebrew word rendered *train up* can have a unique and little-known meaning. In the days when Proverbs was written, the term may have been used to describe a practice done right after birth in which the mouth of a baby was cleared to allow breathing. The chaplain indicated that if this meaning is in view here, we could understand this term as meaning "create an environment for life."

So the verse essentially means this: *Create an environment for life for a child according to his individual gifts and bents, and when he is old he will not depart from it.*

One of the most awe-inspiring aspects of becoming a parent is the realization that you are your child's first teacher and greatest influencer. From the moment of your child's birth, your imprint is made on this tiny, miraculous human being God has entrusted to you. Your attitudes, your behavior, your decisions, your reactions—those are some of the first lessons you're teaching. Your child is watching, listening, and absorbing what you're saying and how you're saying it. Whether your son or daughter was born to you or grafted into your family by adoption, your home and family become the core of his or her life, the source of safety and security. It is a sacred trust.

You teach your children how to hold a spoon, how to walk, how to talk, and how to avoid danger. You use instruction and discipline to help them distinguish right from wrong, bad from good. You model what their priorities should be, and you teach them to recognize and resist temptation.

You quickly discover that those "individual gifts and bents" make each child unique and sometimes unexpectedly challenging. With each successive child, you realize there are also no one-size-fits-all parenting techniques. Most of all, you understand that children are definitely not going to make your life convenient.

But you also begin to understand—amid the chaos, the mess, and the exhaustion—that you have the privilege of rearing and nurturing children who can change the future, and even perhaps the world. Every individual is created by God for a purpose only he or she can fulfill. And part of your purpose as a parent is to instill in your children character, integrity, and a heart for God, their creator.

In the greater scheme of things, you don't have a lot of time to do it. There are roughly 960 Saturdays between birth and high school graduation. The time you spend with your kids is brief and precious.

WHAT ABOUT SCHOOL?

In November 2022, the NEA (National Education Association) released this tweet on social media: "Educators love their students and know better than anyone what they need to learn and to thrive."[1]

This statement somehow "misspelled" the word *parents*. No one knows better than *you* what your children need to learn and thrive. In fact, allowing educators to take over the role of parenting can have devastating consequences.

As your children develop—physically, mentally, emotionally, and spiritually—you make many critical decisions about how and what they learn. When it's time for them to start formal schooling, you need to ask yourself some key questions about each option you consider:

- Is my children's safety the top priority?
- Will those who teach them honor the moral and spiritual beliefs I've instilled in them?
- Will their uniqueness be recognized and valued?
- Does it matter to the educators what friends my children choose?
- Do I have a good grasp of what's being taught in the classroom? How accessible to parents are the curriculum and the policies?

And the most important question of all:

- Will I relinquish control over these issues, on a day-to-day basis, to an educational system that may or may not agree with my core beliefs?

WORLDVIEW MATTERS

If yours is a Christian family, it's important to you that your children grow up with a biblical worldview, with God and His Word at the center. God is the standard for truth, and we look at everything through the lens of Scripture. If you send your children to a Christian school, you expect that the biblical worldview will be integrated into every subject and that students will be surrounded by teachers and staff who put God first.

But what about public school? You may have always thought that public schools do their best to remain neutral in terms of worldview in order to objectively teach literacy and other core academic subjects. And perhaps that's still true in some local areas. But on the federal level, the Department of Education and the teachers' unions are definitely *not* neutral.

In December 2018, the NEA published an article entitled "'Education Is Political': Neutrality in the Classroom Shortchanges Students." What do they consider neutrality? The article quotes assistant professor of teacher education Alyssa Hadley Dunn as saying that "education, at its core, *is* inherently political." The article also states: "The kind of neutrality that concerns Dunn is, for example, a decision to avoid discussion of 'controversial' issues—racism, inequity, climate change, or gun violence, for example—out of fear of appearing political or partisan."[2]

Assistant professor Dunn was part of conducting a larger study:

The study concludes that teacher training programs need to better prepare educators in adapting their classrooms to help students understand current events and political upheavals. . . . [U]ltimately, teachers are charged with preparing their students to work toward a more democratic society. . . . And while too many parents still believe the classroom door should always be shut to any political discussion, they may be "ignoring the reality that such a move is never really possible," Dunn says.[3]

You may have compelling reasons to send your child to public school. But before you do, go in with your eyes wide open. Stay involved. Stay informed. Stay knowledgeable about what your child is learning and which textbooks and curriculum materials are being used. Remember: Worldview matters, and there's a big difference between a biblical worldview and a secular humanist worldview. Your children will spend eight hours a day being taught the public school's worldview.

> Worldview matters, and there's a big difference between a biblical worldview and a secular humanist worldview.

THE WAKE-UP CALL

In 2020, parents all over America received a jarring wake-up call about their children's education. As a result of the pandemic lockdowns, it was suddenly required that all students switch to remote learning at home. After an initial chaotic scramble to provide equipment and internet access and a frantic flurry of activity rearranging work schedules and childcare, something huge that had been hidden for decades began to be revealed.

Parents and caregivers started to take notice of what was on their children's computer screens as they watched their teachers teach and interact with students. And an overwhelming number of parents discovered that they hadn't been paying enough attention to what was being taught in their children's classrooms.

Most parents believed that public education taught the basic academic subjects, that the majority of teachers were highly qualified, and that everything centered on the students who were being educated. They thought they could trust public schools to do what's best for their children. But as it turns out, in many cases that simply was not true.

"U.S. students consistently score lower in math and science than students from many other countries. According to a Business Insider report in 2018, the U.S. ranked 38th in math scores and 24th in science."[4]

And in November 2022, even more disturbing details were revealed: "According to a Gallup analysis of data from the U.S. Department of Education, there are about 130 million adults in the U.S. who have low literacy skills." The analysis also revealed the following:

- Fifty-four percent of Americans between the ages of sixteen and seventy-four read at below the sixth-grade level.
- According to the Project for Literacy, the average American reads at the seventh- or eighth-grade level.
- One in four children in the United States grows up without learning how to read at all.
- Two of three students in the United States who can't read properly by fourth grade end up on welfare or in jail.[5]

What have the public schools been teaching if not the basics of literacy? Academic instruction has taken a back seat to social justice and the sexuality and gender identity of children.

In the fall of 2016, teachers in Seattle public schools created one of the first Black Lives Matter at School events despite controversy over the issue of political activism in education. Since then, this program has spread into thousands of schools throughout the country.[6]

The program's website describes the organization as "a national coalition organizing for racial justice in education." They go on, "We encourage all educators, students, parents, unions, and community organizations to join our annual week of action during the first week of February each year."[7]

The program offers curriculum materials that provide classroom activities for kindergarten through twelfth-grade students based on the Black Lives Matter movement's

"13 Guiding Principles." Here are just three of those guiding principles:

- "We are committed to disrupting the Western-prescribed nuclear family structure requirement."
- "We are committed to fostering a queer-affirming network."
- "We are committed to being self-reflexive and doing the work required to dismantle cis-gender privilege and uplift Black trans folk."[8]

Specific examples of what to say to students are included in the curriculum. For instance, here is what they suggest elementary teachers tell their students: "Everybody has the right to choose their own gender by listening to their own heart and mind. Everyone gets to choose if they are a girl or a boy or both or neither or something else, and no one else gets to choose for them."[9]

This is indoctrination, plain and simple, instilling in young children an anti-biblical worldview. Such curricula are already widespread through our public schools, and their use continues to grow.

In case you still believe that public schools are primarily teaching academic subjects, or that you as a parent have the exclusive right to teach your kids about sex and gender, consider this statement from Planned Parenthood claiming that *they* will educate all children, from kindergarten to high school graduation:

As a respected leader in sex education, Planned Parenthood delivers programs, resources, and tools in classrooms, communities, and online that help people make informed choices about their sexuality and relationships, so they can lead full and healthy lives. We are committed to advancing the health of young people in this country by providing comprehensive sex education that is medically accurate, culturally responsive, equitable and accessible—as well as inclusive of varying gender identities, expressions and sexual orientations.[10]

WHAT ABOUT ALL THE GOOD TEACHERS?

There are thousands of good teachers in public schools scattered throughout the United States, and there are many *exceptional* teachers—some amazing educators who break out of the mold and boldly blaze new paths. My early classroom teaching career was spent entirely in public schools, and I was privileged to work side by side with several great teachers. But I quickly found out that the public school system is stacked against the educators who want to make their students the top priority. Teachers actually have little control over curriculum and administrative policy. And most have no choice but to join and pay dues to the national and local teachers' unions.

These teachers love your children, but they have serious limitations placed on them with respect to class size, discipline measures, parental involvement, and opportunities to help children individually. Your children, during the course of their kindergarten through twelfth-grade education, will sometimes get a real gem—a teacher they'll remember for the rest of their lives. But it's likely that most of the time your children will be taught in traditional schoolrooms by teachers who must juggle their full-time work and family life while complying with a lot of institutional and union regulations, both political and social.

Even the most qualified and loving teachers in public and private schools still have to teach many students the same things at the same time and in much the same way. It's not realistic to expect them to personalize and individualize their teaching styles to accommodate the way each student learns. This is one of the best reasons to stay in touch and support your child's teacher whenever possible so that you can find ways to help your child be an active participant in his or her own learning success.

WHY ARE WE STILL SENDING OUR CHILDREN TO PUBLIC SCHOOLS?

Why are we still sending our children to public schools? Some of these sentiments may sound familiar:

- *If we can just get him through school . . .*
- *He's barely skating by, but I think he's going to graduate.*
- *She hates school, but she only has to make it four more years.*

- *I'm just looking forward to some kid-free days.*
- *Well, maybe next year she'll get a better teacher.*
- *This emotional roller coaster is normal for middle-school kids.*
- *I already pay for public school with my taxes. We sure can't afford private school, too.*
- *I didn't like school either. He'll survive.*

When you send your children to public school, you are trusting that those who teach them—for six or more hours per day for 180 or more days per year for at least thirteen years—will continue to instill in them the attitudes, behavior, and beliefs you have so carefully planted. You are also accepting that your children will spend the same amount of time with friends and peer groups who will deeply influence what they believe and how they act. But once you begin to see what the not-so-hidden agenda really is, you may want to seriously reconsider your options.

As Christian parents, we have to take back the education of our children. It won't look the same for everyone. But we must no longer take someone else's word for what and how our children are learning. What you may have taken for granted in the past when it comes to public schools, private schools, or even homeschooling may have now shifted in ways you didn't see coming. You may believe that your alternatives for educating your children are limited by money, location, or your own knowledge and abilities.

But what if you could make sure that your children not

only have the best opportunities for success in their education but also the ability to become confident, lifelong learners? What if you could have more control over their spiritual and emotional learning? And what if your children could be the most important part of this whole process?

Teaching isn't simply pouring information into a child and then testing them to see if they learned the information. It's not about giving them an education and sending them on their way. Attendance and homework and good grades don't really mean anything if students don't know how or why they learn.

If we're just trying to get our kids through school and out into the world, we're missing the point. Who will care about them more than you do? Who will instill in them good values, a strong work ethic, and a spiritual and moral compass?

This book will provide you with an abundance of practical ideas and strategies for making lifelong learners of your children. It will introduce you to a world of possibilities and give you confidence if you decide to break away from the default option provided by the government. But even if you ultimately decide to keep your children in public school, you'll find solid, proven ways to equip them to take responsibility for their own success in learning.

> If we're just trying to get our kids through school and out into the world, we're missing the point.

Many things in this world are beyond your control to change, but there are also some powerful things you *can* change. This is a book full of hope for your children's futures! We want to offer you immediately useful ways you can teach them to be everything God wants them to be. When it comes to instilling motivation to learn, it's always best to get your children involved in their own solutions and success.

This book could be your game changer.

BITE-SIZED TRUTHS

- Teachers aren't working with blank slates—children are bringing what they've learned from their parents.
- Your children often know more about what's going on than you think they do.
- There will be sacrifice involved in your children's education— but make sure it's not your children who are being sacrificed.

Problem:
One-Size-Fits-All Education

A SCHOOL BUS STOPS at the corner in front of our home every school morning at 6:05 a.m. Two adolescent boys get on an already full bus and head for school. Between three thirty and three forty-five in the afternoon, those boys are dropped off at the same corner in time to go do their homework for the next day.

Even speaking as an early-morning person, I can't imagine having to wake up, get dressed, eat breakfast, and walk to the corner before six o'clock every morning.

But that's how our public schools work. In fact, that's been the routine for a long time. Technology and innovation have revolutionized our lives, sometimes at lightning speed. But public education operates nearly the same as it did more than 175 years ago in the model created by Horace Mann.

> Known as the father of public education, Mann developed the American education model based on the Prussian system during the industrial age. The approach is a one-size-fits-all model based on the faulty notion that all students of the same age will learn the same amount in the same length of time, and in the same way. Therefore, students are grouped by age, not understanding level. Subjects are taught one hour a day in isolation from each other, and the focus is on teaching toward the test. The curriculum is fixed and not responsive to what students need or want to learn.
>
> Considering that Mann died decades before the telephone was invented by Alexander Graham Bell, the lack of innovation in K–12 education is astonishing. . . .
>
> Despite more money being pumped into the $800 billion K–12 public education industry each year, learning results continue to slip. U.S. students place 26th among other developed nations, and 77% of students exit 13 years of K–12 public schooling failing to reach proficiency levels in foundational subjects.[1]

WHO GETS TO DECIDE WHAT'S NORMAL?

Most people believe kids go to school to learn, but children don't automatically know how to do that. There isn't usually any instruction on *how* to learn—most of the focus is on *what* to learn. From the beginning, they're told what to *do* (such as sit still, be quiet, do what you're told). The ones who question—those who resist, who don't fit in—are at risk of being shifted into a particular category or given a special label:

- "She has attention-deficit/hyperactivity disorder (ADHD)."
- "He has processing problems."
- "She has several behavioral issues."
- "He needs to be tested for special learning needs."

According to the National Center for Education Statistics: In 2021–22, the number of students ages 3–21 who received special education and/or related services under the Individuals with Disabilities Education Act (IDEA) was 7.3 million, or the equivalent of 15 percent of all public school students. Among students receiving special education and/or related services, the most common category of disability was specific learning disabilities (32 percent).[2]

Sometimes a child's lack of cooperation or conformity even results in strongly recommended therapy or medication. Of course, there are legitimate cases for intervening on behalf of children who truly need help. But what about those who simply struggle with the instructional methods that are being used?

Dr. Thomas Armstrong, researcher, seasoned educator, and bestselling author of *The Myth of the ADHD Child*, offers sobering statistics to support his claim that our nation's schools are in crisis:

> One in ten preschoolers has had suicidal thoughts. Doctors are increasingly seeing children in early elementary school suffering from migraine headaches and ulcers, and many physicians see a clear connection to school performance pressure. A third of our adolescents report feeling depressed or overwhelmed because of stress, and their single biggest source of stress is school, according to the American Psychological Association.[3]

Dr. Armstrong asserts that "each child is an unrepeatable miracle. . . . Yet school all too often takes away that precious sense of individuality (or keeps it from developing) with its emphasis on uniform standards and procedures."[4] A natural question we should ask here is this: If so many students are struggling with traditional classrooms, why aren't we changing the classrooms instead of the students?

Many parents and educators don't realize that the ever-popular label of *ADHD* is not simply a convenient way of categorizing what appears to be a learning problem. It's not a harmless label you put on a child who seems to need an extra boost just to focus on academic studies. It's a formally defined term that describes a psychiatric disorder.[5] This can have lifelong implications by determining failure or success in careers, and it can cause long-term mental, physical, and social alterations. It could potentially attach a stigma that could change your child's self-esteem forever.

There's no definitive, objective set of criteria to determine whether a child has ADHD. It's commonly judged by a set of behaviors, largely caused by what a child is being asked to do and what context he or she has to work within. For example, I'm a restless, just-get-to-the-point person, so in a situation where I have to sit still for an extended length of time while listening to a rambling lecture, I'll be fidgeting, maybe rolling my eyes, sighing, and generally being a bit obnoxious. But if I spend the same amount of time listening to one of my favorite Christian comedians (Tim Hawkins comes to mind), I'm fully engaged and attentive. So before you become convinced that your child has attention-deficit/hyperactivity disorder, ask yourself what you were requiring him to pay attention *to*.

> But that isn't the way God has made us. He has made many parts for our bodies and has put each part just where he wants it.
>
> **1 CORINTHIANS 12:18** (TLB)

CHANGE THE FOOT OR CHANGE THE SHOE?

We already know that each child has individual gifts and bents, so shouldn't we be paying attention to how those affect the way he or she learns? If we simply follow the standard, regimented methods of grouping and teaching and evaluating students, we leave little room for understanding or helping them develop into successful adults.

When you take your children to the shoe store, you have to find shoes that fit. If the shoes don't fit, you can't change the feet—you need to keep shopping until you find the right shoes. When it comes to school, however, we offer few styles of "shoes." If children's feet don't fit, we force them into the shoes and insist that they wear them anyway.

Many students are forced to wear shoes that don't fit. And as soon as they can, they take them off and never want to learn again. Some people tell me that even in corporate settings they avoid taking classes or doing extra training. They remember too well how that shoe felt in school. How can we justify making children suffer a boring and sometimes painful educational experience if it makes them never want to learn again?

We can keep accountability and maintain standards of achievement while still finding shoes that fit each pair of educational feet. But if we keep making learning a dreaded chore to be done or a prison sentence to be served, we shouldn't be surprised if each successive generation becomes less and less interested in doing it. However, if our goal is to help every child succeed, then we must help each child discover his or her own natural

> How can we justify making children suffer a boring and sometimes painful educational experience if it makes them never want to learn again?

learning strengths and use those strengths to overcome limitations and achieve success, even if those strengths are at odds with traditional classroom demands.

TEACHING THEM TO LEARN

A few years ago, Dell Technologies and the Institute for the Future released a report stating that 85 percent of the students in kindergarten through twelfth grade will end up in jobs that haven't been invented yet. Their strong conclusion was that the ability to gain new knowledge will be more valuable than the knowledge itself.[6]

Although it's hard to know which specific skills will be needed, the report insists that we can and must focus on new methods of learning. One thing is for sure: It has never been more important for our children to be *learners*—not just students who simply do what is required to pass a test or obtain a diploma. This means that while we're teaching them, we also must be teaching them *how* to learn.

Every life is precious, created by God and worthy of love and significance. Every individual possesses great potential for success, regardless of physical or mental limitations. Discovering inborn strengths and learning how to use them gives a joy and

> It has never been more important for our children to be *learners*—not just students who simply do what is required to pass a test or obtain a diploma.

satisfaction that transcends culture, creed, race, or age. This book will give you the keys to help unlock that potential in each of your children by weaving learning into the very fabric of their lives. And in the process, you'll discover a lot about your own learning strengths as well.

If you want to build confidence, inspire lifelong learning, and equip your children to handle hardship and failure, get them involved in their own solutions for success. The next few chapters will give you some highly practical ways to do that.

BITE-SIZED TRUTHS

- It's important to teach children *how* to think, not just *what* to think.

- Traditional school does not seek to discover or honor a student's unique, God-given strengths.

- There is no magic or perfect environment for every student to learn in.

PART TWO

Teaching Your Child to Learn in Any Academic Setting

A Simple Formula for Success

Be agreeable, be sympathetic, be loving, be compassionate, be humble. That goes for all of you, no exceptions. No retaliation. No sharp-tongued sarcasm. Instead, bless—that's your job, to bless. You'll be a blessing and also get a blessing.
1 PETER 3:8-9 (MSG)

I'VE LOVED MY LITTLE SISTER from the beginning, when she was too young to argue with me, and now we're close friends as grown-ups. Some of the years in between, though, were a little rough. We argued and sniped at each other until it almost drove our mother crazy. But one day, when I was almost thirteen and my sister was almost eight, our father made an announcement that changed everything.

Dad was a preacher, and he had just attended a particularly meaningful training weekend that highlighted the power of positive thinking. As soon as he walked in the door, he gathered the family together and made a pronouncement. "From now on," he said, "we are all going to be positive thinkers."

As he explained what that would involve, he zeroed in on my sister and me. "And beginning now, every time you say something negative to or about your sister (or anyone else), you'll have to put a dime from your allowance in this jar."

Oh boy. My small allowance disappeared entirely before the week was over. So Dad came up with an alternate plan. Every time we said something negative to each other, we would have to follow it with three positive things. I quickly discovered that "I like how you tie your shoes" did not qualify as one of the three.

Dad suggested that we look at the strengths in each other and point those out if we were going to criticize what we didn't like. In the short term, both my sister and I discovered that we often simply refrained from saying something bad, since we didn't want to follow it with three compliments. In the long term, though, we learned that even those who irritated us had some good traits that helped balance the negative.

That same principle can be applied to discovering how our children learn and what they need to succeed when they're struggling.

MEASURING SUCCESS

In the 175-year-old model of traditional school, the school day is divided into subjects, usually taught in isolation, each for an hour or so per day. Every student must take the same required classes with limited opportunities for specialized electives that might hold sincere interest. Mastery of the subjects is usually measured by grades, and grades are almost always determined primarily by tests.

Here are some common statements you might hear from students:

"I'm terrible at math."

"I love English, but my science grade is really bad."

"History is my worst subject."

"I wish I could just do art all day."

To obtain a high school diploma, students must have a minimum grade point *average*, which means that with the grades for every class they love and excel in, they have to average in the lower grades from the classes they dread. Even if they work hard, do all the homework, and understand a subject, unless they can get a good grade on the test, they're considered to be deficient. It's easy to fall behind, and many get so discouraged that they just want to give up.

Over the years, the federal government has developed special learning programs, counseling, and therapy to help students cope with what they term *learning disabilities*. In 1975, the Education for All Handicapped Children Act (EAHCA) was passed, which recognized the need for special-education services for those who were diagnosed with learning disabilities. In the 1990s, it was renamed the Individuals with Disabilities

> Even if they work hard, do all the homework, and understand a subject, unless they can get a good grade on the test, they're considered to be deficient.

Education Act (IDEA). In the beginning, it appeared to be a lifeline for children with severe physical and mental disabilities, allowing them to participate as normally as possible with their peers.[1]

If you look up the more recent description of IDEA, however, you'll find that the medical definition in the *Diagnostic and Statistical Manual of Mental Disorders* states this: "Specific Learning Disorder . . . includes difficulties in reading, written expression, and mathematics."[2]

According to the National Institutes of Health (NIH), learning disabilities are disorders that affect one's ability to understand or use spoken or written language, do mathematical calculations, coordinate movements, or direct attention. Although learning disabilities occur in young children, these disorders are usually not recognized until a child reaches school age. Research shows that 8 to 10 percent of American children under eighteen years of age have some type of learning disability.[3]

Although many children can benefit from effective special-education interventions, I have to wonder if we're a little too quick to presume that a child's struggle to pay attention or become proficient in math is automatically a disorder. And if we're declaring that learning disabilities occur in young children, how do we know how much of their behavior has to do with the normal development of their unique learning strengths?

As adults, we're not expected to do everything well. We choose our interests, our careers, and the skills we want to develop based on what we're drawn to or what we want to gain more confidence by acquiring. Some of us excel at using entrepreneurial creative instincts, for example, but there aren't many classes or tests in school that measure such things. Theoretically, school is designed to be preparation for adulthood. But if we're focused on pointing out weaknesses or discouraging children to do out-of-the-box thinking, we might find ourselves surrounded by adults who believe they're just average or even deficient in some way.

USE YOUR STRENGTHS

My first year of teaching was at a public high school in rural Idaho. I was hired to teach the subjects I loved—literature, grammar, spelling, and speech. I was fresh out of college, so I was only four years older than the seniors in my classroom. I was excited to teach, and I was sure they'd be excited to learn. But they weren't.

Several of the teenage boys were amused by my enthusiasm. "We don't need all this English and spelling and writing and stuff," one of them said. "We're just going to be farmers."

Another boy piped up. "Yep—and we're already pretty good at that."

I paused, then smiled. "What is it that makes you good farmers?"

They proceeded to regale me with their skills, weaving in the arts of milking, branding, feeding, and harvesting.

"Well, I'm totally a city girl, but that all sounds really impressive," I told them. "You need a lot of discipline to get up that early, and you sure have to know your land and animals. But do you also have to do business with other farmers and buyers?"

"Of course," one boy replied. "We sell cattle, and Rick's family sells wheat and barley."

I nodded. "So when you talk to buyers about getting the best price for your product, would it help to appear smarter than you actually are?" They grinned. "I can teach you how to talk and write so that no one will ever know you hated having to take English. Just give me a chance to prove it."

I can't say that they were ever truly *excited* about it, but they did give me a chance, and almost every one of those boys got at least a B in my English class. It turns out that the strengths that made them good farmers also helped make them better students.

YOU CAN ONLY BUILD ON STRENGTHS

It's easy to point out weaknesses, but you can't build anything using them. You can only build on strengths, and with a little practice, you can get really good at finding learning strengths in yourself and your children. Unlike with the isolated subjects taught at school, you can help your kids recognize how a strength in one place can also be used in another. It's easier to criticize yourself for not being able to do something than it is to think of three good things about you that might help you get past your difficulty.

For example, Marie complained that she just couldn't memorize the words for a spelling test. "I'm *terrible* at memorizing!" she wailed.

Her mom put her arm around her shoulders and said, "Marie, do you know what I like about you?"

Marie looked surprised and shook her head.

"Well, you're one of the best encouragers I know when it comes to cheering up your friends and helping them with their frustrations. Suppose you call one of them who also has trouble memorizing and study with her for this test? Quiz each other back and forth until you've both got those words down pat!"

> You can only build on strengths, and with a little practice, you can get really good at finding learning strengths in yourself and your children.

Marie accepted the challenge, and she and her friend both aced the spelling test.

A great verse to memorize with your kids is James 1:12: "Anyone who meets a testing challenge head-on and manages to stick it out is mighty fortunate. For such persons loyally in love with God, the reward is life and more life" (MSG).

THE FORMULA FOR SUCCESS

Regardless of where or how you decide to educate your children, there's one absolutely critical thing you need to do: teach them how to recognize and use their strengths to be confident learners. It's not as daunting as it may seem at first. There's a simple, straightforward formula for becoming a successful learner, and you can use it for yourself while you teach it to your children:

THE FORMULA FOR SUCCESS

1. Know your strengths.

2. Figure out what you need in order to succeed.

3. Be ready to prove it works.

1. *Know your strengths.* Sometimes you just need to sit down and work through a few questions that will get you thinking about what you need to really be at your best.
2. *Figure out what you need in order to succeed.* It may take some trial and error, but by deliberately trying different methods, you can begin to form a plan for how to face almost any learning challenge.
3. *Be ready to prove it works.* Accountability is always necessary. You don't get to use your learning style as an excuse for failing to learn. But you may be surprised at what actually works.

Remember: Learning that is meaningful enough to last a lifetime is a result of having the motivation to learn in the first place. You're going to love this journey!

The next three chapters will help you recognize what it takes to be at your best—what your strengths are in key areas of learning—and also identify those strengths in your children. These chapters introduce quick, easy, and practical ways to tackle almost any academic challenge. We may not be able to count on the educational system changing significantly in the near future—that will take a lot of time and incredible resolve. But in the meantime, we can equip our children with the confidence to recognize what they need to do to succeed in any academic setting.

BITE-SIZED TRUTHS

- Teach your children to be watchful for new opportunities to learn—to ask questions and pursue truthful answers.

- Sometimes the most difficult and resistant learners are the ones who change the world.

- The traits that give you the most success in life may be the ones that got you in trouble in school.

4

What Helps You Concentrate?

If you wait for perfect conditions,
you will never get anything done.
ECCLESIASTES 11:4 (TLB)

WHERE ARE YOU RIGHT NOW as you're reading this book? I can tell you where I am as I write it: in my comfortable recliner in the living room, laptop on my lap, music (sometimes TV) on in the background, with iced tea and a snack nearby and diffused light in the room, surrounded by notes, files, and piles of paper.

Some of you are cringing or shaking your head in disbelief. Others are nodding, feeling totally comfortable with my description. *But knowing where, and in what conditions, you're best able to concentrate on a task is a key tool in being able to learn in any academic setting.*

My husband, in contrast to me, is in his office, working at his desk, overhead light on, shades wide open to let in natural light, door closed to outside distractions. We live and work in the same house, but our workspaces are completely opposite.

Which one of us is "normal"? How much influence does the physical environment have on our concentration and productivity? We will both tell you that it has a *lot* to do with it. One person's distraction is another person's inspiration. Each of us has trouble imagining how the other can possibly concentrate in the situation he or she has chosen. But both of us can prove that it works. This is one example of knowing your strengths and figuring out what you need to succeed.

> One person's distraction is another person's inspiration.

SHOULD YOU BE FLEXIBLE WITH YOUR KIDS?

After a parenting seminar, one frustrated mom cornered me: "My son wants to do his homework lying on his stomach on the floor with headphones and music on while eating potato chips and drinking a soda pop. That's just ridiculous—no one can study like that! But we argue about it constantly, and I'm so tired of fighting with him. What can I do?"

I gave her the same advice I've given to hundreds of other moms: As long as he's not breaking any household rules, tell him you'll let him study for the next three school nights the way he wants to. If the homework is done correctly and turned in on time, simply say, "Well, I could never do it that way, but as long as you're proving it works, you can do it."

If, on the other hand, the homework doesn't get done, or isn't done correctly or on time, at the end of those three days say, "Nice try. Doing it this way obviously doesn't work. Let's adjust things until we find an approach that works."

This answers two important questions:

1. What's the point? (The point is that the homework gets done correctly and is turned in on time.)
2. How many ways are there to get the job done? (Remember, one person's distraction is another person's inspiration.)

This approach works for many issues. And by allowing your child to try something, you're shifting a lot of the responsibility to them to figure out what's going to work, which is an opportunity for them to grow.

Whether you're teaching your children at home or supervising them while they do homework from school, you may be surprised at how much easier and more effective it can be if you encourage them to create their ideal space for concentrating and getting the work done. You can get some hints on what they like by watching where and how they get comfortable in their leisure time. Let them experiment with some variations and see what choices they make. The bottom line is still proving that their approach works.

My twin sons, Michael and Robert, look so much alike

that at first glance most people would assume they are much the same in everything. But they are almost totally opposite, and they always have been. In fourth grade, when it came to doing homework, Michael had to be at a table by himself in a quiet place. Robert, on the other hand, worked best lying on his stomach on top of the coffee table, waving his legs in the air. Both boys got their homework done on time, but they took very different approaches.

YOU CAN'T ALWAYS BE COMFORTABLE

While most people see the value in having a place to relax and feel comfortable, many will tell you that being at school is not one of those places. Again, the 175-year-old public school model lends itself to straight rows, hard chairs, individual desks, and a strictly controlled environment. Even the majority of private schools usually duplicate this teaching-and-learning environment. It's the rare school, public or private, that deviates much from the original model.

Does the physical environment really make a difference in how kids learn? It turns out that not only does it affect children and adolescents while they're in school, but it can also have a lasting effect on them as adults. "[Researchers] point out that the number of school-aged children and adolescents reporting frequent episodes of back and neck pain and headache has increased in the last few decades and that it is now recognized that people suffering during childhood are likely to suffer back pain in adulthood too, unless the problem is treated appropriately."[1]

The lighting in the average classroom also causes student discomfort and constitutes a health threat:

> Scientific studies from recent years have shown that lighting can significantly affect how well students perform in the classroom. For example, if lighting is too dim, or if it flickers overhead, students may have trouble focusing and retaining information. Poor lighting can also affect the health and well-being of teachers and faculty. School staff members may feel tired, sluggish, or unmotivated to teach, which negatively impacts students' performance levels. . . .
>
> Outdated fluorescent bulbs commonly flicker and become dim, which is thought to cause eye strain, headaches, and discomfort for both students and faculty.[2]

Although technology and research are beginning to make significant changes in the workplace with improved desks, chairs, and lighting, most school classrooms are still stuck in the early twentieth century.

CAN A CLASSROOM BE MODIFIED TO WORK BETTER FOR EVERYONE?

Several years ago, I worked with a Christian high school teacher who was determined to improve her students' attention and achievement by changing the classroom. Mrs. M said, "These kids are restless and inattentive, constantly look-ing for a reason to get up, to walk around, and to get a hall pass for the bathroom."

We surveyed all 120 of Mrs. M's students in her six class periods combined. We asked them what made them espe-cially uncomfortable or distracted during class. They were quick to tell us.

What were the main issues?

- The desks were the kind that are attached to the seat, so some of the taller or bigger athletes had to stretch out their legs, often pushing against the desks in front of them.
- Unless students were petite or particularly slender, when they got up from their desks, the desks came with them.
- The surfaces of the desks were small and had little room for both notebook paper and a book.
- The outdated ceiling panels with fluorescent lighting cast a harsh, artificial light, making it hard to concentrate and often causing headaches for some.
- The concrete walls were cold and unfriendly.

Mrs. M understood their complaints, but the school had no budget to make any modifications. So she and I asked her 120 students to participate in an experiment. We gave them three questions:

1. What is the point of paying attention in class?
2. What are the top reasons it's difficult?

And the most important question:

3. If we find a way to change the classroom, do you believe you can prove it works?

I made some suggestions for how the classroom could be modified to accommodate different learning styles. But I told the students that before I made a budget and figured out a way to pay for it, they had to prove that the changes would not only result in their paying more attention but also significantly improve their participation in class discussions and their work on in-class assignments. If at least 90 percent of the 120 students would sign a pledge that promised this outcome, we would find a way to adjust the physical environment to address their complaints. Ninety-five percent of the students signed the pledge.

It took almost four months, lots of persistent prayer, and a huge miracle to pay for it, but the classroom transformation was complete before spring break that year. When the students walked in on that first day after the work was done, they found several four-foot tables instead of desks. Each student had an office chair (minus the wheels) that swiveled and adjusted for height. The glaring fluorescent lights had been diffused with panels that filtered the light without dimming it, changing the whole room into a calmer space. The walls were covered with bulletin boards and decorated with the school logo.

Mrs. M and some of the school administration braced themselves for the students gleefully having a free-for-all, spinning the chairs, and going a little crazy. But that's not what happened. After a few minutes, the initial novelty wore off, and students discovered how much easier it was to concentrate in class. Instead of getting up multiple times, most just swiveled back and forth quietly at their tables. As they worked, they all had elbow room and space to have a book or supplies at hand. Over the course of the next few days and weeks, Mrs. M kept a record and reported back: "The kids come into my room and take a deep breath when they sit down. They say this is the only place they look forward to coming to in the whole school building."

And did the students prove that it worked? Mrs. M tracked their progress, and by the end of that quarter, she observed that almost every student had improved. And it turned out there was a bonus—a distinct reduction in noise and discipline problems.

Despite the success of the project, other teachers and schools resisted following the same course. Many commented that it was great but not practical. It just seemed too daunting to many of them. They cited budget concerns, possible lack of control over the students, putting too much focus on student comfort and not enough on the serious academic setting, and so on.

Fortunately, there are administrators and teachers out there who would be open to the possibilities of redesigning classrooms. Perhaps you know of one. And if you're willing to help them accomplish it, you could improve the lives of a lot of students.

LET'S FIGURE IT OUT

There's a saying that seems true for pretty much everyone when it comes to learning: *The brain can only absorb what the seat can endure.*

When you're uncomfortable physically, it's difficult to concentrate on or pay attention to anything else. By getting a handle on what your child ideally needs, you can find ways to adapt and adjust when necessary.

On the following pages is an informal survey for helping your child identify some of the elements in his or her physical environment that can affect concentration. (As you fill this out for them, try also filling one out for yourself.) Get your child as involved as possible with input on this; draw on your own observations where necessary. (A student workbook is also available as a free download. To access it, scan the QR code on the last page of this book.) Of course, there will be times when the situation will not fit natural preferences at all, but awareness is half the battle. When your child recognizes why she's having difficulty paying attention or focusing on work, it's somehow easier for her to endure it. After all, it's not that something is wrong with her—it's a matter of figuring out what it's going to take to succeed in spite of the circumstances. That's a valuable life skill.

> The brain can only absorb what the seat can endure. When you're uncomfortable physically, it's difficult to concentrate on or pay attention to anything else.

Your Personal Profile

Place a mark on each continuum above the description that best fits.

TIME

When it comes to being at my best when learning,
I am more of a

| morning person | (no preference) | night owl |

Whenever possible, do your hardest things at your best time of day and your easiest things at your worst time of day. This one change alone can almost double your productivity.

DESIGN

In order to be at my best when studying or working,
I need an environment with a

| classic, formal design | (no preference) | informal, relaxed design |

If you have to work in an environment that offers the opposite of what you need, look for small, discreet modifications you can make. For example, you can buy inexpensive seat pads or a lumbar cushion to put behind your back. Some teachers will allow a child to use a seat pad that rotates as long as it doesn't distract other students and they can prove they're paying attention in class.

LIGHTING

When concentrating or learning, I need

subdued lighting   (no preference)   bright lighting

If you have no choice of lighting but do have a choice of seating, try looking for a corner of the room where the light makes it easier for you to concentrate.

INTAKE

In order to be at my best when studying or learning, I

am distracted by   (no preference)   need to
eating or drinking   eat or drink

Most school classrooms won't allow eating and drinking. But sometimes just putting a piece of hard candy discreetly in your mouth will temporarily satisfy the need for intake. If nothing at all is allowed, try to have a quick snack or drink right before class.

TEMPERATURE

In order to concentrate when studying or learning, I need

a cool   (I can adapt)   a warm
temperature   temperature

Most people can adapt to a room's temperature by putting on or taking off a layer of clothing, like a sweater. For those especially sensitive to the extremes, it's a good idea to come prepared for the worst and be braced for anything. Remember, awareness is half the battle. Knowing what you're up against somehow makes such issues less daunting.

THE EARLIER THE BETTER

Besides doing this survey with your children, take it a second time with your own preferences in view. The sooner you can get a handle on your own strengths and bents, the better you'll be at helping your children figure out theirs. Encourage experimenting whenever possible, and challenge your children to come up with solutions that work—both in ideal situations and under frustrating circumstances.

Knowing what I know about myself now, I would have been so happy if my parents could have afforded to buy a used restaurant booth and put it in my bedroom. Sitting in a comfortable seat with snacks and drinks at hand in a nice, cool room with people nearby but not talking directly to me—who knows what I could have accomplished!

BITE-SIZED TRUTHS

- It's important to teach children the difference between *I need it* (which often just means "I want it" or "I would prefer it") and *I can't work successfully without it.*

- Help your children own their own success—don't do their work for them.

- Don't expect the system to accommodate you. The only way things are going to change is if you prove that certain changes produce positive results.

5

What Helps You Remember?

"Are you listening to me? Really listening?"
MATTHEW 11:15 (MSG)

"OKAY, CLASS. Today we're going to talk about animal cruelty."

Instantly Corey's hand shot into the air. "Oh! Oh! My aunt—she had this dog—"

"Corey, we don't have time to listen to everybody's stories right now. If there's time at the end, you can tell us all about it."

Corey froze for a moment. His aunt's dog story was right on the tip of his tongue. In fact, it was all he could think about. If he didn't tell someone right this minute, he'd forget it. He quickly turned to the kid next to him and told him the story. Whew! Now he had room to listen to what Miss Rogers was saying.

But it was too late. He was once again in trouble for inappropriate socializing.

According to Corey's parents, he's been this way his whole life—and this is only the third grade. His mom is especially worried, since she was the kind of student who never talked out of turn or got in trouble with her teachers. How was Corey ever going to learn if he talked all the time?

The thing is that Corey is smart—really smart. But he usually learns best—and remembers what he's learned—by talking and asking questions. In other words, he's primarily an auditory learner.

This leads to another key tool for your child to use in achieving success in any academic setting: knowing and accommodating what approach best helps him or her remember what has been taught. We'll look at auditory learners first, and we'll soon consider visual and kinesthetic learners.

AUDITORY LEARNERS

You might think that auditory learners would need to listen, and that's true. But the need is not to listen to others talk; it's to listen to *themselves* talk. They need to hear their own voice say something in order to remember it. So they ask questions, interrupt, and seem to talk more than they listen. They may even talk to themselves under their breath without realizing it.

When an idea occurs to them, they might just blurt it out before they've thought it through. Then, once they've heard themselves saying it, they can adjust or change their minds as they go. They may make a "thinking noise" as they work or play, not even realizing others are listening.

Auditory learners may read more slowly than others, even when they're excellent readers. This is usually because they're saying each word in their head as they go without skipping any. In the classroom, they may talk to other students just to find out what everyone else is thinking.

It's not easy for auditory learners to sit quietly and listen at school. It's important for them to be able to ask questions or talk their way through a thought process. They tend to get in trouble most often for not raising their hands before they answer questions or for talking too much to their neighbors.

Not long after my husband (Jack) and I (Cynthia) were married, I realized just how auditory Jack is. This especially showed up when we watched a movie at home. Not far into the movie, Jack would say something like "Do you think that dog is going to end up helping them find their way back?"

> It's important for auditory learners to be able to ask questions or talk their way through a thought process.

I'd push the pause button until he finished talking and then start the movie again.

A few minutes later, he'd say, "See? I just wonder if they have the dog there so they won't get lost."

I'd push the pause button again, because I knew he wouldn't want to miss any words in the movie. Then I'd push play again.

Sure enough, after just a few more minutes, he'd interrupt again, and I'd pause the movie again. Before he could finish his thought, I'd protest, "Jack, if we keep having to pause, it's going to take forever to watch this movie. I can't concentrate on the story if we keep stopping to talk."

And Jack would reply, "If I can't talk about it, I won't be able to understand what's happening."

So we came up with a solution. For each two-hour movie we watch, Jack gets three pauses—no judgment, no questions asked, no complaints from me. But after the third pause, he has to be done interrupting. This helps both of us. I have more patience and understanding for his need to talk, and he disciplines himself to interrupt less often. Sometimes I see him open his mouth to talk but then change his mind. (This usually happens when he's only got one pause left and wants to save it for something more important.)

VISUAL LEARNERS

Ears that hear and eyes that see—
    we get our basic equipment from GOD!
PROVERBS 20:12 (MSG)

This proverb is true on multiple levels. For example, unlike Corey and Jack, some of us are *visual* learners. I'm a preacher's kid, and I went to a Christian college. I was eager to take a Bible class, thinking it would be easy to get a good grade. But the year I did, my professor had decided to grow a beard that made him look like Moses. He was short, and the beard reached almost to the ground. It was pretty scraggly, and the whole time he talked, he stroked and scratched and fiddled with the beard.

I was mesmerized. I couldn't take notes. Surely something was hiding in that beard, and if I looked down to write something, I'd miss seeing it drop out. I got a C when I should have gotten an A.

I wish I had known then that I'm a highly visual learner. I'm drawn to what I see, and whatever I can't see, I try to visualize. I have an active (even overactive) visual imagination, and I'm easily distracted, disappearing into my imaginary world at a moment's notice.

Visual learners are often more interested in what they can see than in what you say. When they hear a teacher giving directions, for instance, they're waiting to see an example of what's expected. When they're listening in class, they may draw or doodle to help them concentrate. Rather than getting in trouble for talking, visual learners tend to get graded down for not talking. This is sometimes described as "lack of participation." One teacher found that if she handed out blank sticky notes, her visual

> Visual learners are often more interested in what they can see than in what you say.

students could be encouraged to write down their comments or questions and stick them on the door as they left the room.

Here's a classic example of the difference between an auditory mom and her visual daughter:

Mom: "Sweetie, I need you to go to the kitchen and take the blue mug by the sink outside to the patio table."

Daughter: "Okay." (As she turns to walk away, she already can't remember what her mom just said. But she doesn't want to ask, because she figures her mom would then say "Weren't you listening? How many times do I have to say it? Why don't you pay attention?")

So the daughter goes downstairs and tries her best to guess what she's supposed to do, and it usually doesn't turn out well. But suppose the conversation went like this:

Mom: "Sweetie, I need you to go down to the kitchen and get the blue mug that's sitting by the sink." (Pause.) "You know, that bright blue porcelain mug?" (Another pause.)

Daughter: (Thinks for a moment, then her face brightens.) "Oh, yeah, that new blue one."

Mom: "Well, I need you to take the blue mug outside to the white table on the patio." (Pause.)

Daughter: "Okay!"

And everything usually turns out well.

Visual learners need to picture it as they go—not just listen to the whole thing at once. In school, they tend to get in trouble for not following verbal directions or for doing what looks like daydreaming when the teacher is talking.

> We ask you—*urge* is more like it—that you keep on doing what we told you to do to please God, not in a dogged religious plod, but in a living, spirited dance.
>
> **1 THESSALONIANS 4:1** (MSG)

KINESTHETIC LEARNERS

One Christian school in Arizona has a unique fourth-grade classroom. If you walk in during their computer lab, you'll find several of the students sitting on large exercise balls while intently working at their computers. Their bodies are constantly moving, adjusting to keep their balance on the balls, but they don't even seem to notice. If you ask their teacher, Mr. R, about it, he'll tell you that when they're finished, they'll move over to their desks to continue the school day.

Mr. R had a particularly restless group of students one year, and from what he knew about kinesthetic learners, he recognized that their constant need to move was seriously interfering with the requirement to sit still for any length of time.

He met with the principal and the parent association and asked if he could try an experiment. If the parents would provide their children with large exercise balls, Mr. R would allow the students to use them as their chairs as long as they could prove that it would result in better and complete assignments. Out of the initial ten students who tried it, six proved that it worked for them.

When the kinesthetic learners had to sit still in chairs, their minds were preoccupied with only one thought: moving. When their bodies were moving on the exercise balls, however, their minds no longer had to worry about moving. Instead, they were able to concentrate on the tasks in front of them. Most of the time, they didn't even realize their bodies *were* moving.

It's easy to spot kinesthetic learners. Not only do they seem to be in constant motion, but they also struggle with waiting. For example, if they have to wait for the Walk sign at the intersection, they may keep pushing the button until it changes. An elevator button may already be lit, but they need to push it a few times themselves anyway. If you're a teacher and insist on giving long instructions, you may find that they mentally check out or start on the project or assignment before you finish talking.

> When the kinesthetic learners had to sit still in chairs, their minds were preoccupied with only one thought: moving.

They don't necessarily take others' word for things. Something may be true for you, but how do they know it's true for them? The vending machine has an Out of Order sign taped to it, but is it really? You said that the food tasted bad, but maybe it's just you. The sign on the door says

Danger: Do Not Enter, but what if you just want to know what the danger *is*? One thing is for certain: Kinesthetic learners don't give boredom a chance to overtake them.

> You made all the delicate, inner parts of my body
> and knit me together in my mother's womb.
> Thank you for making me so wonderfully complex!
> Your workmanship is marvelous—how well I know it.
> **PSALM 139:13-14 (NLT)**

LET'S FIGURE IT OUT

Every person has strengths in all three areas: auditory, visual, and kinesthetic. Usually, the younger we are, the easier it is to identify them. As we mature, we find ourselves using all three when we need them, but we still tend to have a favorite. Again, awareness is half the battle. Recognizing what our children's strengths are can help us communicate with them more effectively and can help them figure out what works best when they're trying to remember information.

If you're not sure which approach is best for your child, try asking these questions:

- *What are you thinking?* (auditory)
- *Do you see what I mean?* (visual)
- *What should we do about this?* (kinesthetic)

As before, fill out the profile on the following pages for both your child and yourself.

Your Personal Profile

Place a mark on each continuum above the description that best fits.

Auditory: To remember something, I usually need to hear myself say it out loud, discuss it with others, or make a "thinking noise."

AUDITORY

When it comes to remembering information, I use my auditory strength

| a lot | sometimes | never |

- Ask me questions.
- Tell me what you want and let me ask questions.
- Use emphasis and emotion in your voice; no monotone.

Visual: To remember something, I usually get a picture in my mind and then draw, doodle, or write it down.

VISUAL

When it comes to remembering information, I use my visual strength

| a lot | sometimes | never |

Show me something as soon as possible.
- Give me a chance to visualize what you're saying.
- Put it in writing whenever you can.

Kinesthetic: To remember something, I usually need to move around, take short breaks, and take some kind of action.

KINESTHETIC	When it comes to remembering information, I use my kinesthetic strength		
	a lot	sometimes	never

- Let me do something as soon as possible.
- Go on a walk or do something with me while we talk.
- Get to the point quickly.

BITE-SIZED TRUTHS

- Children are not meant to make your life convenient.

- Get your children involved in their own solutions and success.

- You can be a partner in your child's learning. No one expects you to know it all.

6

What Helps You Understand?

Make a careful exploration of who you are and the work you have been given, and then sink yourself into that. Don't be impressed with yourself. Don't compare yourself with others. Each of you must take responsibility for doing the creative best you can with your own life.

GALATIANS 6:4-5 (MSG)

WE WERE DRIVING on a rural road on our way to a conference when Jack and I had a life-changing experience. We drove by a house that caught my eye—it looked like a cartoon house. It was shaped like a small castle, with four turrets, each one painted a glaring fluorescent shade of green, pink, yellow, or blue. The blinding flash of color and eccentricity startled me. As we passed, I said to Jack, "Can you believe that house?"

He replied, "Yeah. How much would you pay to cut down that tree?"

I blinked at him. "What tree?"

He turned to me and asked, "What house?"

"Wait. Are you kidding me? How could you have not seen the house?"

We both agreed we had to turn around and go back. And there it was—a huge, ugly, sprawling monkey tree in front of the house. Oh, wow. How could I have missed it? Jack said, "Oh, that *is* a weird house," and I said, "That's the ugliest tree I've ever seen."

We shook our heads and laughed. What an unmistakable illustration of how opposite we are! For the first time, we got a clear picture of how truly strong each of our filters is when it comes to how we perceive and understand the world. I honestly didn't see the tree. He didn't even notice the house. To this day, if we're in the middle of a disagreement, sometimes he'll stop and say "What house?" and I'll reply "What tree?" and the tension will break as we both laugh.

As you can probably tell, I married someone who is almost completely opposite to me when it comes to understanding and communicating information. Chances are good that a lot of you reading this book did the same. In the beginning, did you think it would be a refreshing perspective? You may have noticed since then, however, that on a day-to-day basis—no matter how much you love the person—it's just *not* that refreshing. After all, isn't each of us living proof that our way works?

As it turns out, God has a plan to deal with this—and it involves the realization that we really do need each other. It's like the right and left hand. If the right hand insists that the left hand be exactly like it (if that were even possible), you couldn't do much with two right hands or two left hands. We have one of each for a reason. Each hand encounters the world from an opposite perspective, but together they make a beautiful team.

PRE-WIRED

Some of the most important and enlightening research about how opposite minds take in and understand information was done in the 1940s by Dr. Herman A. Witkin. Initially, he began his work as a contractor for the US military, but he soon expanded his research to include studies from around the world. The following labels (*analytic* and *global*) have been adapted to give us a more understandable description of the technical terminology.

Roughly half the world's people were born with wiring that makes them more analytic when it comes to learning and processing information. In other words, when information comes in, their minds are automatically hardwired to immediately *look for details, focus on specifics, break it down,* and *organize it.* They usually want to figure out what they're supposed to do and then efficiently get it done. They like an orderly process and a predictable working environment.

The other half of the people could be categorized as more global, meaning *big picture, putting things in context,* and *looking at the whole before getting the details.* They seem naturally more intuitive and more in tune with the people around them than the information in front of them. They tend to look for the overall gist of what you're talking about, which usually translates into wanting someone to just give them the general idea and then let them deal with details as they go. For globals, work environment can be fluid, and they often thrive on flexibility and spontaneity.

Knowing whether your child is more analytic or more global and helping her recognize and apply that insight to her learning are keys steps toward your child's finding success in any academic setting.

WHAT AM I?

No one is completely analytic or global. Every person has both kinds of strengths and abilities. But we don't have an even balance of both; virtually everyone is tipped toward one end of the spectrum or the other. This built-in wiring goes across culture and gender. Some of us are more extreme than others, and most of us can stretch and adapt when we really need to. But let me repeat what should by now be a familiar phrase: Awareness is half the battle.

This is a basic and structural framework that indicates how your mind takes in, processes, and makes decisions about information. Naturally, it affects the way your child learns and, to a great extent, how successful he or she will be in a traditional school setting. Although there are exceptions, the overwhelming majority of school classrooms and teaching methods are a better fit for the more analytic students.

There will be times when you can switch back and forth easily between the analytic and global perspectives and times when you just feel like you're in the middle. For purposes of illustration, though, let's look at a few highlights that show the contrast.

> The overwhelming majority of school classrooms and teaching methods are a better fit for the more analytic students.

Analytic Learners

Strengths

- doing things in order
- working independently
- focusing on details

Things That Frustrate Them

- a sudden change in plans
- not having clear directions
- being forced to work in a group

Global Learners

Strengths

- getting a general sense of things
- working together with a partner or team
- making others feel understood and appreciated

Things That Frustrate Them

- too much routine
- working alone
- working without inspiration

Are analytics smarter than globals, or vice versa? No. Decades of solid, empirical research and testing of these two opposite learning-style strengths have found no difference in intelligence between the two groups. In other words, both types of students are smart, capable, and full of potential. The biggest variables lie in the methods of delivering and receiving information and the instruments for measuring how well academic performance has been achieved.

What follows are some examples of how analytics and globals do things differently (though both achieve academic success).

STAYING ORGANIZED

It's common to be graded on how well you keep your notebook and desk organized. Most analytic students are not shaken by this—it makes sense to them to sort and organize their assignments and keep track of handouts and other materials that need to be preserved. Analytics may especially take pride in the neat and attractive appearance of their notebooks and systems of keeping track of things. Even when they're using electronics, there's a distinct difference in how many icons are laid out on their desktops.

The globals, on the other hand, may start out strong—especially if their notebooks can be personalized and have an appealing color and design. But it doesn't take long for the organization part to lose ground. That's when files turn into piles. After all, there's a lot going on, and it's not as if globals have time to do anything but stuff those papers in their notebooks while on the run. They'll set aside some time later for sorting and putting it all back together again.

The problem is, there's never really a good time to sort and organize. It's all there, you understand—it just doesn't *look* very put together. And when a teacher suddenly pops a surprise inspection of notebooks, globals are in trouble.

Many parents struggle with their children over this organization issue. However, whether it's a disorganized notebook or a messy bedroom, there *is* a good way to get your global to be truly organized. Namely, give them a standard they can meet that accomplishes the purpose of being organized.

Let's go back to the basic question: What is the point of being organized? Answer: So you'll be able to find what you need when you need it. When I was teaching, I told my students I'd be grading their notebooks and organization systems based on one test: They had to be able to find and deliver anything I asked for in sixty seconds or less. If they could do that, they were organized. If they couldn't, they had to change their system until they could. I never ceased to be amazed at what some of those notebooks and systems looked like—and yet students usually proved that their ways worked.

STAYING MOTIVATED

One of the biggest differences between analytic and global minds is what drives them to succeed. Analytics work well with the traditional approach to goal setting and achievement: Define the goal, decide what they need to do to achieve it, and get it done so they can do what they want to do.

It's not that clear with globals. Who made this goal? Why is it important to achieve it? Can it be done by working as a team? Can we change it if we need to?

I remember figuring out this difference with my twin sons, especially when they got into upper elementary school. Homework was always an issue, but each boy had a different idea of what it would take to get it done. Mike, the analytic, wanted to work at a table, alone, without interruption. He was determined to get his work done without stopping and then reward himself by having some leisure time before bed.

Rob liked the idea of getting the homework out of the way, but he struggled with where and when to do it. Obviously, Mike didn't want him to sit at the table, but Rob hated to work alone. He could do it for a few minutes, but then someone else in the household would pass by and seem to be having a lot more fun, and he would "take a break" and promise to come back and finish later.

One thing that worked to solve this issue was setting aside a block of time when everyone in the family worked on things at the same time. Whether it was balancing the checkbook, reading a book, or working on a crossword puzzle, we all focused on a task that needed to be done. Our global son, at least for a short, concentrated period, could focus on getting his homework done.

FOCUSING ON ONE THING AT A TIME

More analytic learners often insist on finishing one thing before going on to another. Although this makes sense to minds that prefer the step-by-step, neatly ordered approach, the more global thinkers are almost always going to struggle with that practice.

One way to explain it is this: Globals operate best by bursts of inspiration followed by long plateaus of nothingness. If they have multiple projects going, when they hit a plateau, they can temporarily switch to a task that's more inspiring.

True, it may drive analytics working with them crazy to have multiple different projects going at the same time, but again, *What's the point?* Globals may bump right up against the last-minute deadline, and everyone around them may have to endure a flurry of panicked activity. And if the deadline is missed anyway, they must endure the consequences. If you are parenting globals, help them recognize why meeting deadlines may be difficult for them, and encourage them to find solutions—perhaps working with other people, talking to their teachers to get more specific information about what needs to be done, and so on.

> The global approach can be messy, undefined, and variable.

Both analytic and global students need to recognize and understand the opposite points of view, and both will benefit from knowing what the end goals are, even if they get to them by different means.

WHAT ABOUT SCHOOL?

You can probably imagine which kind of learner has the most difficulty with the traditional school structure and grading criteria. From the beginning, school has been largely analytic in nature. It's easier to measure and administer education if you use standards and procedures that are uniform and produce charts, graphs, and statistics that are consistent and quantifiable. The global approach can be messy, undefined, and variable. The one-right-answer viewpoint is much easier to measure than the but-what-if questions that inevitably come from global minds.

Being aware of this is helpful in and of itself. But imagine how much more productive education can be when it takes into account the minds that are getting educated. Accountability should always be required. But what if the *What's the point?* question gets asked and answered enough to figure out different ways to get to the same end goal?

> Get along among yourselves, each of you doing your part.
> Our counsel is that you warn the freeloaders to get a move on.
> Gently encourage the stragglers, and reach out for the exhausted,
> pulling them to their feet. Be patient with each person, attentive
> to individual needs. And be careful that when you get on each
> other's nerves you don't snap at each other. Look for the best in
> each other, and always do your best to bring it out.
>
> **1 THESSALONIANS 5:13-15 (MSG)**

You can start to think through what this looks like by filling out the profile on the following pages both for your child and for yourself.

Your Personal Profile

Place a mark on each continuum above the description that best fits.

Analytic: Focus on specific facts; break information down piece by piece; remember details.

ANALYTIC

When it comes to understanding information, I use my analytic strength

| almost always | sometimes | almost never |

My Preferences
- ☐ having an orderly process
- ☐ knowing what to expect
- ☐ being objective and fair

My Frustrations
- ☐ having plans change suddenly
- ☐ not knowing exactly what I want
- ☐ being forced to work in a group

Here are some questions analytics could ask when encountering teachers or situations that are just too global:

- *Where is a good place to start?*
- *How long do I have before this is due?*
- *How will I know when I've done this the right way?*

Big picture/global: Focus on the big picture; get an overall understanding of the "gist of things" in context.

When it comes to understanding information, I use my big-picture, global strength

almost always   sometimes   almost never

My Preferences
- ☐ spreading things out to see everything
- ☐ feeling understood and appreciated
- ☐ flexibility and variety

My Frustrations
- ☐ having to explain myself
- ☐ not knowing the end result
- ☐ having to work alone

Here are some questions globals could ask when encountering teachers or situations that are just too analytic:

- *Could I work with a partner on this?*
- *Would you look at what I've done so far and tell me if I'm on the right track?*
- *May I see an example of this kind of project (or assignment) that got an A?*

BITE-SIZED TRUTHS

- One of the greatest gifts is the gift of being understood.

- We don't learn as a community; we learn as individuals who then contribute to the community.

- You are not pouring information into your child; you are inspiring your child to search for and acquire knowledge. You're in this together.

7

Putting Children First

Be prepared. You're up against far more than you can handle on
your own. Take all the help you can get, every weapon God has
issued, so that when it's all over but the shouting you'll still be on
your feet. Truth, righteousness, peace, faith, and salvation are more
than words. Learn how to apply them. You'll need them throughout
your life. God's Word is an *indispensable* weapon. In the same
way, prayer is essential in this ongoing warfare. Pray hard and
long. Pray for your brothers and sisters. Keep your eyes open. Keep
each other's spirits up so that no one falls behind or drops out.
EPHESIANS 6:13-18 (MSG)

"BEFORE I AGREE TO TAKE YOU AS A CLIENT, you must guarantee me that you are willing to lose everything—your home, your possessions, your career, your reputation, *everything*—in order to keep your children."

I (Cynthia) sat in my divorce attorney's office, listening to words that couldn't be more foreign. I looked at him.

"Do you really think I'll have to—"

"Yes," he interrupted. "I think there is a very strong possibility that what I just told you will become necessary."

I swallowed and nodded. "Absolutely. I'm willing to do whatever it takes."

The moment was surreal. The unthinkable was happening. It was a day I will never forget. After seventeen years of marriage, an unexpected and unwanted divorce suddenly thrust itself into my life. It involved some jarring discoveries and potentially threatening situations for my children. And now it was clear that they were my top priority.

The boys were twelve years old. I ended up being a single mom for four years, and I came very close to losing everything that was less important than my children. Financially, emotionally, vocationally—I experienced true brokenness in all those areas. I had to make some deep financial sacrifices to keep the boys in the beloved Christian school they had attended since first grade. But my relationship with God was never stronger, my commitment to my children never deeper. His provision and guidance were never clearer, and my faith grew several sizes during that period. (I am now married to a wonderful, godly man who has partnered with me in life to create a future and a ministry I could not have sustained alone. I am truly blessed.)

I don't know what your situation is or has been, but I do know that in God's plan He gives us children so we can step outside ourselves and invest our lives in something that will outlast us. As you make decisions about how and where you will bring up your children, it has never been more important to do your research on the options available to you. And ultimately, when it comes to education, *teaching your kids to learn in any academic setting boils down to putting them first.*

A vital part of our parenting is teaching our children to cope with what's hard for them, but one of the biggest keys to success is how you teach this. Remember, you can only build on strengths; a solid foundation cannot be built on weakness. Know each child. Appreciate their differ-

A vital part of our parenting is teaching our children to cope with what's hard for them.

ences. Look for ways to bring out the best in them, using their natural strengths and abilities. Teach them how to recognize what they do well, and challenge them to use those strengths to tackle problems and situations that don't match their natural preferences.

DAILY MINIMUM REQUIREMENTS

Let's do a quick review of the learning-style strengths covered in this book. But first, remember that no two children are alike, and what helps one learn may not be the best approach for another. Although there's no magic formula and no one right way to do this, getting a grasp on key issues can make a big difference.

I call a person's learning-style strengths *daily minimum requirements* because using them is like taking vitamins to keep your mind and body healthy and fit. They're based on the premise that it's easier to keep people healthy than it is to try to make them well once they're sick. Children need to learn to cope with the inconvenient, the unexpected, the less-than-ideal parts of life. But they do a better job of that when they come at it with the confidence of knowing what it's like when they are at their best.

If you have to do what doesn't come naturally day after day, there may come a breaking point, a crisis, and you may not have the reserves to cope. On the other hand, if you recognize what's going on, you can stretch on purpose, knowing you're okay and you just need to step outside your comfort zone to get this done.

Daily Minimum Requirements

Auditory Learners

Need to talk.
Need to ask questions.
Need to hear from you.

- Can they tune in to the tone of your voice and your expressiveness when you speak?
- Will they be able to ask questions?
- Can they talk about what they're learning?

Visual Learners

Need to see what you're talking about.
Need to show you what they mean.
Need to have time to watch and think.

- Can they make regular eye contact with the person teaching them?
- Can they watch and interpret facial expressions?
- Can they "see" what you mean?

Kinesthetic Learners

Need to keep moving.
Need to get to the bottom line quickly.
Need to take action.

- Is there at least some freedom of movement?
- Will there be something to do besides listen?
- Can they do something with what they learn?

Analytic Learners

Need routine and predictability.
Need organization and procedures.
Need to work on one thing at a time.

- Will the rules be enforced consistently for everyone?
- Will the expectations be clear and not need extra explanation by the teacher?
- Is there a chance to excel individually?

Global Learners

Need to be valued as part of a team.
Need flexibility and chances to be spontaneous.
Need to multitask to capitalize on inspiration.

- Will they be able to work cooperatively?
- Will they know they are loved and valued for who they are?
- Can they find inspiration in what they're learning?

PUTTING YOUR CHILDREN FIRST
IN THE CHOICE OF SCHOOLING

Part of putting your children first in the pursuit of making them lifelong learners is to consider carefully where and how they're going to be schooled. Recall, for instance, that public school teachers have less and less control over what and how they teach. Academic excellence is often overshadowed by social justice, liberal politics, and gender identity issues. As you read in the first chapter of this book, the sexualization of even very young children is becoming more common. No matter how wonderful a school or teacher may be, it's still important to stay vigilant, do your research, stay involved in your child's day-to-day activities, and find ways to support and encourage the teachers who are committed to your biblical worldview.

Christian schools can be a great option to consider, but they are not all the same. You still need to do your due diligence in confirming whether the school you are considering is a good fit.

If your child is in a Christian school, be as involved as possible—use your strengths and talents, and make yourself available to help wherever you can. Find ways to encourage and support the teachers and staff.

If you have the financial means, perhaps you can even help create scholarships for families who can't afford to send their children to private school. Many Christian schools are offering to come alongside parents who can't afford full-time tuition but want their children to have a strong biblical foundation for their education. Some have programs that offer a blend of traditional school and homeschool, making a Christian education more accessible.

If your children attend public or private school from pre-school to high school, they will be away from home most of the day for at least 180 days a year. That's roughly 50 percent of fourteen years that they will spend their days being taught by someone else. Where and how they spend that time is a critical choice you must make.

Will the moral and spiritual values of your schooling choice line up with yours? Will your children be valued as unique and capable individuals who don't have to fit neatly into the same box as every other student? Will their peer group be made up of the kinds of friends you want them to have? Will they be taught solid academics and not be indoctrinated politically and/or morally? These are just a few of the questions you'll want to have answered before you sur-render half of their childhood to school.

TODAY'S HOMESCHOOL SCENE

I've asked Mary Jo Dean, co-founder of Great Homeschool Conventions with her husband, Brennan, to contribute the next two chapters so you'll have a better handle on what the possibilities are when it comes to taking charge of your chil-dren's education. You'll love their personal story, and you'll be encouraged by Mary Jo's success at homeschooling her own three children (now successful adults).

You may have at least briefly considered the option of

homeschooling or a hybrid form of it. You may not have realized how many versions and variations of homeschool are available today. If you haven't explored what that landscape is like these days, I believe you'll be surprised and encouraged to find out how practical and rewarding it can be.

Most importantly, pray and seek God's guidance for where and how you should be educating your children. The stakes are higher than they've ever been, and you'll never regret the time you spend making sure your children's foundation is strong.

In his devotional *My Utmost for His Highest*, Oswald Chambers reminds us of the importance of not only what we do with our lives but also how we make an impact on the world through our children: "We cannot measure our life by success, but only by what God pours through us, and we cannot measure that at all."[1]

> Pray and seek God's guidance for where and how you should be educating your children. The stakes are higher than they've ever been.

BITE-SIZED TRUTHS

- Teach your children to pursue truth and practice wisdom—they may not get that in school.

- Teach them self-control and self-discipline—their teachers can't do that for them.

- Teach your children to be men and women others can trust and believe in.

PART THREE

The Homeschool Option

8

Why Would You Homeschool?

Mary Jo Dean

With all this going for us, my dear, dear friends, stand your
ground. And don't hold back. Throw yourselves into the work of
the Master, confident that nothing you do for him is a waste of
time or effort.

1 CORINTHIANS 15:58 (MSG)

A GREAT SURGE OF FAMILIES decided to try homeschooling
in 2020 when the public schools switched to remote learning
in place of in-person attendance. In fact, data from eighteen states reveal an increase of 63 percent in homeschooling
families in the 2020–2021 school year. Even more striking
is that after the return of in-person learning for 2021–2022,
the number of families homeschooling decreased by only
17 percent.[1]

One article on the phenomenon said, "Families that may
have turned to homeschooling as an alternative to [public
schools'] hastily assembled remote learning plans have stuck
with it—reasons include health concerns, disagreement with

school policies and a desire to keep what has worked for their children."[2]

Another article quotes Josephine Herr, a mother of four in Kansas City and one of the homeschool moms who decided to keep doing it: "Our boys were academically struggling in school. We knew we had to do something and slowly build their foundation back up, along with the freedom to choose what best met their learning style. . . . My favorite [part] is how I'm learning alongside my children and seeing the boys master something they've struggled with." Herr also adds that her children "love the flexibility of their schedule" and says, "We go year-round and take breaks whenever we feel like it. I love the idea that my kids can get their work done by lunch or even [enjoy] a four-day school week."[3]

One mom in Raleigh, North Carolina, said she began homeschooling her seven-, ten-, and eleven-year-old children when "the school system's shortcomings became more evident" to her: "My kids have a lot of questions about different things. I'm like, 'Didn't you learn that in school?' They're like, 'No.'"[4]

And as one mother commented in one of our Great Homeschool Conventions surveys, "My husband and I have raised many children over the years. We are still raising three grandchildren we adopted. We have homeschooled for the most part, but we've also done some public school, private school, blended school, and so on. We have never been sorry for homeschooling, but we have regretted some of the public schooling."

"I COULD NEVER HOMESCHOOL"

I (Mary Jo) was raised in church and accepted Jesus as my Savior at an early age. And He has been my source of comfort, grace, and never-ending love all these years. In 1989, I met Brennan, and nine months later we were married.

Today, we have three amazing adult children. Our older son graduated from the University of Cincinnati and works in the data analytics field. Our second son graduated from Miami of Ohio, where he played football, and then went on to graduate from the University of Pennsylvania Carey Law School. And our youngest went to Mount St. Joseph University, where she received her undergrad degree and a master's degree in reading and gifted education.

> Looking back, I never would have imagined the adventure we've been on. And I sure never would have imagined I would be a homeschooling mom.

But if you saw where we started, you would never have guessed that that's how we'd end up. Not in a million years. And looking back, I never would have imagined the adventure we've been on. And I sure never would have imagined I would be a homeschooling mom.

IF WE COULD DO IT . . .

My husband and I both came from modest backgrounds. I say that not to pat ourselves on the back but rather to encourage you that if we could do it, *you can also homeschool successfully!*

I grew up in a middle-class, blue-collar family in a small Kentucky town. My mom was a high school graduate, but my dad dropped out of school prior to finishing eighth grade. He joined the Marines as a seventeen-year-old and fought on Okinawa in WWII. He returned home to work hard, raise a family, and have us in church almost every time the doors were open.

I attended a large public school and ultimately graduated with around 380 other students in my class. I never really liked school. I was an average student, mainly getting Bs and Cs, though if I really applied myself, I could pull off an A.

It was important to my parents that all eight of their children got a high school education. But since money was tight, if we wanted to attend college, we would have to pay for it ourselves. When I found a good job out of high school making pretty good money, my dreams of going to college were put on the back burner.

I met the love of my life in my twenties. Two years after marrying, we welcomed our first son. Two years after our first, we welcomed our second son. Three and a half years later, our daughter arrived. And in 2023, we celebrated our thirty-third wedding anniversary.

Brennan grew up in a conservative (Wesleyan Methodist) preacher's home. Neither of his parents was a college graduate, and his dad pastored a couple of small churches in Michigan and Ohio—churches whose limited resources required that the pastor also work a full-time secular job.

My husband grew up in a home without a television but with a mother who read to him and his younger brother a great deal. Brennan describes himself as a voracious reader growing up—biographies, historical fiction, the Hardy Boys, Louis L'Amour, and more.

Brennan would say, too, that he was often less than a model student in high school (a bit bored and a bit rebellious) and again in Bible college (mostly out of boredom). Midway through his sophomore year of college, he dropped out and never went back.

So Brennan and I both came from modest backgrounds, and none of our parents had college degrees. Neither did the two of us.

When our first child was born, I quit work to stay home with him. (Eventually, I stayed home with all three children.) We had to cut a lot of expenses, and one of them was cable TV. My children grew up with little TV. In the early years, I would read to them all the time. I would read during quiet time. I would read while they played with their toy cars. I read to them always.

One night when Brennan was working late, I read for so long that I fell asleep while reading aloud to the kids. My son shook my arm and said, "Mommy, Mommy, what happened next?" As I struggled to refocus my vision, I glanced at the clock. I had been reading for four hours straight. As hard as I tried, I could not focus on the page. The suspense of "What happened next?" would have to wait until the next day.

When our older son was five, we put him in kindergarten. While his classmates were learning to recognize numbers, my son was working on two-digit addition problems. He loved math. The teacher took me aside one day to tell me that my son was bored and didn't want to sit still, usually during math time.

I asked the teacher, "If I put math worksheets in his backpack, would you give them to him during your 'counting session'?"

She told me she couldn't do that because my math sheets were not approved. (It's math—what's not to approve?) That's when I realized that no one at the school really cared specifically about my son and his learning. I'm not blaming the teacher—every day she had two half-day kindergarten classes and many students to attend to. She didn't have time to invest individually in my son to maximize his learning and keep him from getting bored.

At the same time Brennan and I began grappling with this reality, we were also wrestling with how to best raise our children with a proper foundation of faith in Jesus Christ and a biblical worldview. Not only is public school not neutral, but it's decidedly anti-Christian . . . and more brazenly today than ever before.

As a single-income family, we couldn't afford Christian-school tuition. We contemplated my returning to work full-time to pay for Christian school, but those budget numbers weren't adding up either.

At first we didn't even want to consider homeschooling. Brennan was concerned about the overall socialization of our children. He didn't want them cut off from what he felt were healthy and necessary opportunities to play sports, participate in clubs, and so on. (Note: There are many homeschool sports teams throughout the US, and many states also allow homeschoolers to play sports in the school district in which they live.)

At the time, Brennan was working in the Christian music business and was around a few people who had homeschooled their kids successfully. A couple of families at our church homeschooled as well. So we did some further investigation and decided to give it a try.

I've mentioned that neither of us has a college degree, let alone training as teachers. Neither of us would describe ourselves as very organized either. And we were about to take on homeschooling our children.

I was nervous. I sure didn't want to mess up our kids. And I knew that this homeschooling endeavor was going to be almost completely *my* homeschooling endeavor—my husband worked long hours. However, looking back, my husband is quick to say that you simply can't overestimate the love and commitment of a "mama bear" who is looking out for the well-being and education of her children.

So we buckled up and started our homeschooling adventure.

In the beginning, I was wide-eyed with excitement that my children would be with me all day. What could be better than spending the entire day with your kids? I purchased a curriculum all of us could do together, and we took many field trips connected to the curriculum. It was wonderful!

Then within just a couple of years, I realized that my oldest was really smart and needed more. Now what? It wasn't long until the wide-eyed excitement turned to tears and frustration. We tried an expensive curriculum in hopes I could use it with all three kids. Nope. They were all intelligent but very much individuals, and they learned differently from each other. Eventually, however, with a lot of trial and error and much perseverance, we got all three through high school.

And that was part of the beauty of homeschooling. I was able to customize some necessary parts of our journey to the specific needs and learning style of each individual child. If we needed a break, we took a break, whether it was for a couple of hours or for a couple of days. We could build in time for a field trip whenever we wanted or needed to. We could go visit their great-grandparents, who lived hours away. Or we could just take breaks at home and read books or play outside.

Our kids played with the neighborhood kids after those kids got home from public school. And we kept our kids involved in church activities, sports, music lessons, homeschool co-ops, 4H, and so on over the years. As they got into advanced mathematics in high school, we also found a fantastic tutor who was a real lifesaver.

I should add that homeschooling doesn't have to be a twelve-year commitment that you make in one fell swoop. When I started, I was thinking in terms of just one year at a time, and that was broken down into doing one day at a time.

My children are adults now, and they will tell you that they loved parts of being homeschooled and disliked other parts. But they are all happy and successful adults, so whether because of our homeschooling efforts or in spite of them, they made it.

Brennan and I compiled our own list of answers to the *Why homeschool?* question. We've frequently listed them on our Great Homeschool Conventions Facebook page:

> The privilege of watching our children grow and learn brings us great joy and fulfillment, and we are not willing to miss that blessing.

- These are our children, and their education is far too precious and desperately important to leave it in the hands of anyone else. It is the most important work we could ever do.
- The privilege of watching our children grow and learn brings us great joy and fulfillment, and we are not willing to miss that blessing, nor are we willing to surrender it to anyone else.
- No one loves our children with greater passion than we do. No one is more committed to their learning than

we are. And no one else could ever come close to being as committed to their receiving a complete, top-quality education that is personalized to their interests and learning styles.

• God has entrusted us with these children, and it is our responsibility to bring them up in the nurture and admonition of the Lord. The ramifications are not only generational but even eternal.

BUT SERIOUSLY, WHY NOT PUBLIC SCHOOL?

We prayerfully and cautiously made the decision to allow our middle child to attend public school for part of his time in high school and our daughter to do so as a senior. (Our oldest was homeschooled through high school graduation.) We thought that, having provided a healthy Christian foundation, we were willing to allow some public schooling, in part as a precursor to our kids' going to secular colleges, with the full knowledge that we could also reverse course at a moment's notice.

I've often heard the argument from Christian parents that there are good teachers in public schools who love Jesus. That's true, but they're exceptions and not the rule. Further, the occasional good Christian teacher has little true power and influence as compared to the agenda of the institution itself—the school district and the teachers' union. *You really must understand that the institution is completely secular and anti-Christian—more so today than ever before.*

I've also heard some parents proclaim that they are sending

their kids to public school to be witnesses for Jesus, to be salt and light in the spiritual darkness that is the public school. I'm reminded of an observation by David French:

> Pastors and families often idealize the public-school experience, calling it a "mission field," and holding out hope that their children can be "salt and light" in a difficult environment. But the process of education largely involves one-way communication, with the teachers and administrators seeing the students as *their* secular "mission field." Isolated young children are more vulnerable than powerful, and I've seen many parents come to grief as fully indoctrinated, peer-pressured kids make mistakes with lifetime consequences.[5]

Pastor and author Paul Washer once said, "Your children will go to public school and they will be trained for somewhere around 15,000 hours in ungodly secular thought. And then they'll go to Sunday school and they'll color a picture of Noah's ark. And you think that's going to stand against the lies that they are being told?"[6]

The late John Taylor Gatto, who taught for more than thirty years and was named both the New York City and New York State Teacher of the Year, had this to say:

> Is there an idea more radical in the history of the human race than turning your children over to

total strangers whom you know nothing about,
and having those strangers work on your child's
mind, out of your sight, for a period of twelve years?
Could there be a more radical idea than that? Back
in Colonial days in America, if you proposed that
kind of idea, they'd burn you at the stake, you mad
person! It's a mad idea![7]

Gatto has great insights, and I would recommend that you acquaint yourself with at least some of what he has written on education. His eye-opening and groundbreaking books include the following:

- *The Underground History of American Education, Volume I: An Intimate Investigation into the Prison of Modern Schooling*
- *Dumbing Us Down: The Hidden Curriculum of Compulsory Schooling*
- *Weapons of Mass Instruction: A Schoolteacher's Journey through the Dark World of Compulsory Schooling*

By the way, I am absolutely *not* suggesting that home-schooling will save your kids. Only Jesus can do that! I *am* suggesting that homeschooling allows you to teach, nurture, and protect your children in critically important ways—generationally important ways—that you simply cannot do when you send them off to public or private school. It also allows you to provide your children with superior teaching tailored to their unique interests, needs, and learning styles.

CHALLENGES

No one expects you to do this alone. And sometimes, for reasons beyond your control, homeschooling just isn't an option for your family. You may find, for example, that there's too much of a personality clash between you and your child. During our research, one mom told us, "My son worked great for the teacher in a classroom, but he just wouldn't settle down and work for me. It was like trying to mix oil and water."

Or perhaps you just don't have the energy and resources to homeschool. I'm not saying it will be easy, even in the best of circumstances. But if you can make it work, it won't always be hard either. Believe me, there are many resources and support groups available to you.

Meanwhile, of course, many of you will look at the financial implications of homeschooling—living on one salary, paying for curriculum and supplies and such when you're already supporting the public schools with your taxes—and conclude you just can't make it work.

If *this* mom could do it, however—with no college education whatsoever and with my own parents having just a high school diploma and an eighth-grade education—you can do it too. And it's so worth it!

BITE-SIZED TRUTHS

- No one knows or loves your children like you do—you have been their number one teacher since they were born.

- Parents don't need to know everything in order to teach. They just need to know where to find the answers.

- Sometimes the most valuable knowledge to have is common sense.

9

Valuable Advice

Mary Jo Dean

Let's keep focused on that goal, those of us who want everything God has for us. If any of you have something else in mind, something less than total commitment, God will clear your blurred vision—you'll see it yet! Now that we're on the right track, let's stay on it.

PHILIPPIANS 3:15-16 (MSG)

GREAT HOMESCHOOL CONVENTIONS is the largest event of its kind in the United States, holding conferences in five regions across the country every year, featuring top speakers, hosting hundreds of workshops and exhibitors, and welcoming more than twenty-seven thousand total attendees. In the fall of 2022, we surveyed almost fifteen hundred parents who are currently homeschooling their children. We asked them, "What advice would you give someone who is considering whether to start homeschooling?"

We broke their responses into three main categories. Here are some highlights from their answers.

WHY SHOULD WE DO IT?

Featured Answers

"Do it. I'm an Ohio school board member, and I see what is being taught in the schools. If you are for Christian values, public/government school is no longer the place for your child. Choose your children's souls over the schools."

"Put yourself in your children's shoes. As an adult, would you tolerate being bullied? Would you tolerate being yelled at? Could you sit quietly at lunch? Remember that children have feelings, and they, too, deserve respect. No one wants to be in a hostile environment. Schools today do not put children first. They put agendas and politics first."

Other Parental Advice

- "When a child departs from the home, [they] will be like [their] teacher. Do you want that to be you or someone else?"

- "In today's society, you just have to make the changes you want for your family. This world is crazy, and for just a little while we can control how much of that crazy affects our children. You can't ruin them, just love them and try your best."

- "Just try it. You can always go back to school if it doesn't work. (Spoiler alert: I believe it will work for anyone who puts the effort in!) But you don't want to look back ten years from now and say 'I wish I had . . .'"

- "Consider that you only get to spend a handful of quality one-on-one years with them. They will be in your home only about one-fourth of their lives."

- "You are capable, and you're not going to ruin your kids. They need you!"

- "When you homeschool, you can better determine what your kids' interests truly are and can open opportunities they would not have had otherwise. You will also know your kids better when you homeschool."

- "You can't do any worse than public school. I know that sounds bad, but what I mean by it is that public schools graduate students who are below grade level in multiple subjects. Kids fall through the cracks or get pushed through for a variety of reasons."

- "Pray about it. Determine whether you want to be the one in charge of education or the one coming behind, trying to counter bad information/values."

- "Don't think about academics more than you would their character. Godly character outweighs knowledge. Our country needs more wisdom, not knowledge."

- "The best thing homeschooling offers is the flexibility to help your children learn the things they want and need to know in the best environment for them to learn those things, without having to replicate all the rules and rituals public/private schools need (and really only use to keep large groups of kids in order)."

- "This is not an educational choice. This is a lifestyle choice. Keep your focus on raising virtuous adults who love what is true, good, and beautiful."

- "If you are thinking about it, then you probably should be homeschooling."

- "Your children will inevitably be shaped by those they spend eight hours a day with for twelve years."

- "Ask yourself if you'd rather teach your kids and pass on *your* values or gamble with them being taught *someone else's* worldview and values."

- "Don't overthink. Kids are naturally curious, and learning happens naturally when we give them time and space to explore their curiosity. The time spent with your child is invaluable, and you won't regret it. You may regret what your children would be exposed to in public school though."

- "It is a sacrifice (of time, effort, potential lost income, money for materials needed), but the investment pays off more than you can ever imagine!"

- "Like marriage, there are some seasons that are blissful and some seasons that are incredibly difficult, but in the end, it is an indescribable blessing. Our whole family has grown together and matured in our faith, as well as in our understanding of God's world. It is a privilege to be the one mentoring my children through all that."

- "Think about the relationships you are building with your children versus the education. In homeschool, we can help raise independent and confident learners rather than successful test takers who fit the mold of public schools."

- "Homeschooling is not only teaching your children; it's also having the privilege of watching them grow and learn right before your eyes. You learn alongside them, so the growing is between you and your children. Just like we get to watch their milestones during the first year of each of their lives, homeschooling lets us continue watching them grow and learn. We get to do life together in every way. What a blessing it is!"

- "Don't make the choice out of fear. Do it for the joy of learning and of enjoying your kids."

- "Homeschool is not just a schooling option. Homeschooling is a lifestyle that allows you to enrich your children's lives and futures. The irony is that we feel that they've taught us more than we could ever teach them. You will not regret more time with your kids learning about life, love, and the pursuit of God."

- "Homeschooling isn't a convenience; it's a lifestyle that requires a lot of love, compassion for all involved, planning, and faith to get through the rough patches. However, the flexibility to teach a child, the amount of knowledge your child can get from a home environment, and the work you pour into supporting their developmental stages is a blessing. . . . [Y]ou get to take some credit for your child's developmental progress, morals, and approach to life—you're raising the adults of the world, after all. The reward at the end of the day, semester, year is typically a well-adjusted child who is always eager to learn and share that knowledge with the world."

- "For every one expected benefit of homeschooling, there are twelve unexpected benefits."

WHAT IF WE DON'T FEEL QUALIFIED TO TEACH?

Featured Answers

"If you have graduated [from] high school or received your GED, you are more than equipped to get your own child through to graduation. The resources and support available are far greater than what our parents probably had access to. You can do it!"

"You don't have to know everything before teaching your child. Learn it *with* your child as you teach it."

Other Parental Advice

- "No one knows your kids better than you; no one loves your kids more than you. Who could possibly be a better teacher to them? Who could want more for them than you? You may not be perfect yourself in all subjects, but you will fight to find them just what they need when they need it. Trust yourself!"

- "God doesn't call the equipped; He equips the called. You can do this! Also, a key part of homeschool success is support! Find support from family, friends, homeschool support groups. . . . There are so many great resources out there, and it's more fun together."

- "If you feel the Lord calling you to this homeschool adventure, don't second guess—just do it! Even if you lack confidence in your own ability, be confident that the Lord knows what He's calling you to do, and He'll equip you for it too. When you can't be confident in yourself, you can still walk confidently in Him!"

- "Prayer with [my] spouse was a game changer. Doors were opened, bringing peace in."

- "You teach your kids from the time they are born. Homeschooling is continuing to do just that. You don't have to know all the answers. You just need an answer key."

- "Bring your child home, enjoy life together, and dive deep into the child's interests. You will be amazed at the development of a student who is not held to the arbitrary milestones of an institutional education."

- "Your role is [to be] the facilitator of your child's education. It's okay to say 'I don't know' and to ask for outside help through tutoring or one-off classes."

- "In [kindergarten through second grade], keep it simple. Academics can happen (with focused attention) in about an hour. Make sure the core subjects happen, but allow lots of time for play and reading aloud. Use part of your day to focus on character, obedience, and life skills, like chores and healthy habits."

- "There is no one right way to homeschool. Do what works for your family. Lean into the flexibility it provides, and trust that the Lord will provide all your children need. He loves them so much!"

- "You can do hard things. You can learn right alongside them. You and/or your family do not have to do this alone. Support, help, and encouragement are there when you need them."

- "Make your goal to create a love of learning. Teach your children to love learning. Some days it's amazing. Others will be hard. I promise it's worth it."

- "Their favorite thing to do is to come home and be with the whole family. We all minister together, love each other, and are close friends. We did life together as a homeschool family, and we still do life together every chance we get."

- "Good parenting is the foundation of homeschool and comes before schoolwork."

- "It is okay to be relaxed. Kids get more from your one-on-one attention than they get out of a classroom lecture."

- "You will quickly realize that you aren't as deficient as you believe yourself to be. The time spent with your children over good books and challenging propositions cannot be replicated elsewhere and is the most worthy of endeavors."

- "Relax, breathe, and study your children. Pay attention to what their specific strengths and weaknesses are."

- "Don't let the thought of homeschooling overwhelm you. You can set your own pace. There is so much support, so you are not alone, and you can do it."

- "You will never regret at least trying."

- "Try not to overthink it. Do what works for your family."

- "Strengthen your prayer life. Pray over everything!"

- "Don't let all the methods overwhelm you. All you need are a few good books and a heart that loves your children. Don't get caught up in the flashy curriculum wars."

- "You know your kids and your boundaries as a parent best. God has given you tools to parent and will give you what you need each day to homeschool. Keep it simple, and take it one day at a time."

WHERE DO WE START?

Featured Answers

"Don't let your homeschool mimic public school. I tried that my first year, and my kids hated it. Go with the flow, don't rush, and have fun. Take breaks when needed. Let your kids find their joy in learning again."

"Don't overthink it. You have been teaching your children since they were born. Turning five doesn't magically change that."

Other Parental Advice

- "Just start somewhere, and gradually add in more things as you get settled into a routine. The number of choices can be paralyzing."

- "If something isn't working, change it. The blessings and benefits of homeschooling will always outweigh the challenges. It's not just about educating your children academically but about embracing the opportunity to experience 'real-life learning' together (parents included). What a gift to have this extra time to treasure and train our children!"

- "Personalize your homeschool according to your family."

- "If possible, try homeschooling for a month in the summer break or in pre-K. (I think you will be surprised.)"

- "Start out small and add more as you gain confidence. It's more important to have a peaceful home than to check everything off a list."

- "Take it a day at a time, and remember: You are not trying to do public school at home."

- "Do it! You can always change your mind if it's not a good fit. You'll build great, lasting memories with your kids while teaching them to love learning."

- "Don't re-create a classroom in your home. Don't expect every day to be a success. Love and enjoy your children. Don't let people who don't homeschool make you doubt what you are doing."

- "Don't try to get everything perfect before starting. Just get started and make adjustments as needed."

- "Find private Christian homeschool support: CHEA [Christian Home Educators Association]; HSLDA

[Home School Legal Defense Association]. Don't [homeschool] out of fear."

- "Tell yourself you will try it for a year and then reevaluate. You'll either love it and keep going or decide that it's not for you."

- "You don't have to do any virtual learning. Socialization— many families have too much on their calendars because there are numerous socialization opportunities with other homeschool families."

- "Just *start* and take baby steps until you establish a routine. It's so much fun to homeschool, and your children will greatly benefit!"

- "Just start simple and make changes as you go."

- "Try it! It doesn't have to be the final decision for your kids' education."

- "Don't go crazy researching. There is enough information out there to be frozen with all the choices. Talk to someone and get started as soon as you can."

- "Don't be afraid to step out and give your child(ren) the best education you can! You as a parent know whether they are understanding the information, and you can advance or slow the learning process for your child. I feel great knowing that my child actually understands what is being presented and is not left behind because he doesn't quite understand."

- "You can do it. The hardest part is getting used to having your kids around most of the time and finding the dynamic that works for you."

- "Short lessons, field trips."

- "Before you try to figure out what you are going to teach, make sure your *why* is clearly defined. Why are you homeschooling, and what do you want to accomplish?"

- "Pray for direction over your decision. Decide first what your educational philosophy is, and then choose a curriculum that matches. Find your people; don't go at it alone. Find a virtual or physical group to be a part of regularly."

- "It will take some time to figure out your child's style and how you want to teach. Go easy on yourself, and focus on the basic things at first. The extras can come later."

- "If you taught your child how to talk, walk, and [go] potty, then you are already a great teacher!"

FEATURED TESTIMONIAL: JENNY'S STORY

Our three children have had a variety of schooling, from a Homelink program (two days a week in class) to full-time public school to full-time homeschool.

I'm so thankful our journey led us to full-time homeschooling. There is such a freedom that comes with it. My husband is able to take the kids on his work road trips and spend quality time with them individually. We also belong to a homeschool co-op that meets weekly. The kids get to pick three classes each, like P.E., volleyball, art, sign language, and speech. This gets us a guaranteed day out of the house to see friends and have some classroom time. The kids love Friday school!

I think it's important to write down your reasons for homeschooling and regularly revisit them. There are definitely hard days and times you will wonder why you're even trying. This is a good time to pull out that list—and then take the day off and take the kids to the park. Don't forget your reasons, and don't forget to pray.

BITE-SIZED TRUTHS

- Homeschool is not simply school at home—don't try to duplicate the school classroom.

- Homeschooling, or some hybrid version of it, can change everyone's life. But you won't know how until you try it.

- It's okay to make mistakes; just let your children see a good example of how to deal with them.

10

Surprising New Options

Let's not allow ourselves to get fatigued doing good. At the right
time we will harvest a good crop if we don't give up, or quit.
Right now, therefore, every time we get the chance, let us work
for the benefit of all, starting with the people closest to us in the
community of faith.
GALATIANS 6:9-10 (MSG)

KELLI HAS BEEN VOTED Teacher of the Year at the Christian
school where she's been teaching for several years. Her tal-
ented and athletic fifth-grade son gets to attend the school
with her, and they both love it. Recently I (Cynthia) asked
her a hypothetical question: "Kelli, if you weren't teaching
full-time at the school and you and your husband decided
your family would be okay with just his income, would you
consider homeschooling your son instead of spending the
money on private school?"

She was shaking her head before I finished my question.
"No way! Sam and I work great together on his homework
or special projects, but he would never make it just having

one teacher—especially if that teacher was me." She went on to explain that Sam, an only child, thrived while spending his days with a variety of classmates, and he was super respectful of his teacher. I asked one more question: "If you had no choice except sending him to public school, would that change things?"

She hesitated. "Yes . . . but I would have to do some serious research about the options. I know there are a lot of alternatives to the old way of homeschooling, where it would just be Sam and me. He needs to learn with other kids, and he loves playing sports and participating in extracurricular activities."

While Kelli's situation worked well for her family, I assured her of the same thing I'm about to tell you: There are more homeschooling options than you've ever imagined. It's not just that there's an amazing array of curricula and materials for all kinds of learning styles. There are also many practical ways to tailor homeschooling to families with all kinds of work styles and schedules.

> There are more homeschooling options than you've ever imagined.

Opportunities for partnering with churches, Christian schools, and charter schools are only the tip of the iceberg. All across the country, you'll find countless forms of co-ops, hybrids, and support groups. Don't just count on a Google search to find them either—start talking to people at your church, join social media sites that share your interest, call your friends, and build a network of support for finding homeschooling options.

The field is wide open for those who have creative and entrepreneurial talents, and the possibilities are almost endless for developing alternatives for parents who want to explore homeschooling practices that fit their family's lifestyle and schedules. There are retired Christian teachers who still love to teach, parents who are experts in a particular field of study or work, and businesses that could provide space or help with a business plan.

A GREAT EXAMPLE

One inspiring example of a successful homeschool organization that helps parents not have to go it alone is found in the heart of the liberal state of Washington. Connections[1] is based in Everett, Washington, and although it had small and humble beginnings, it has been growing steadily since its inception.

Founded in 1994, Connections is a nonprofit organization that provides arts and academic classes from preschool through high school in a supportive, Christ-centered community.

Connections rents space in two large church campuses within thirty minutes of each other, offering multiple classrooms and other large areas. Monday classes are held on one campus and Wednesday classes at the other.

The board of directors, staff, administrators, and leadership teams are all volunteers. Every person on the board has a student in the program and must rotate off when his or her children have left. The minimum period of service requested is two years.

Although Connections is unabashedly Christian, there is no requirement to be a Christian in order to attend, although all families agree to abide by the Statement of Faith and Beliefs while on campus.

The classes are offered as essentially à la carte menu items. There are five class periods from nine in the morning until three fifteen in the afternoon. Students can attend the classes offered on Monday, Wednesday, or both. In addition to offering the in-person classes, the program allows students to attend remotely from other parts of the country. Teachers offer additional online sessions and are available to chat with students to answer questions. The system is similar to a university model and can serve as an element of college prep.

Every instructor is a highly qualified expert. Many of them are certified teachers who have retired or left public or private schools, and all are passionate about the subjects they're teaching. They are interviewed and vetted by the board of directors. Each teacher determines the course content, tuition, and material fees for each class.

The instructors partner with parents to ensure the best level of individual learning for each child. Parents are encouraged to sit in on any of their children's classes they'd like to.

Students are often given assignments or projects to complete at home.

Classes in 2023 included all the academic basics as well as fine and performing arts such as art, band, choir, drama, and other creative electives (History through Games, for example).

There's also intergenerational activity that fosters respect—older kids helping younger kids and teenagers chatting with both younger children and adults.

There are social activities for all the age groups both through Connections and through its sister organization, H.O.M.E. (Home Oriented Meaningful Education)—field trips, service projects, dances, and so on. Many parents and their children say that Connections "feels like family."

Parents have complete control over their children's transcripts and graduation requirements, but they have access to Connections' volunteers, who can assist them with filling out or submitting forms and help parents find the necessary homeschool requirements for their state. Parents also mentor new parents.

Connections continues to grow each year, and God has richly blessed this incredible alternative to public and private schools.

Does this inspire some ideas for you? Is there a similar program in your area?

Maybe you live in a rural community or a smaller city. You may not have access to a program as expansive as Connections. There's no doubt, however, that wherever you live, support groups and options exist that you may not have discovered. It won't take much for you to start exploring the possibilities—and there's no doubt you'll find someone who will be glad to help you!

Homeschool Legal Defense Association (hslda.org) is an excellent place to begin your search. You'll find almost everything you need in a state-by-state format.

IF PUBLIC OR PRIVATE SCHOOL IS STILL YOUR CHOICE

After considering all your options, if your choice is to send your child to public school for whatever reason, you are now better prepared to support that decision. If you've read this far, you know much more than the average parent about how to equip your child to deal with less-than-ideal learning circumstances. Most of all, you are equipped to be as alert and involved as you can possibly be when it comes to what is being taught and who is doing the teaching.

> If your choice is to send your child to public school for whatever reason, you are now better prepared to support that decision.

WHAT TO DO NO MATTER WHAT

Regardless of their method of schooling, your children need you to build a rock-solid foundation at home that includes learning about the Bible, a daily habit of prayer, and conversation about God. Encourage discussion and questions about what they're processing at school and what they're learning. Help them develop coping strategies for dealing with difficult or frustrating circumstances, and challenge them to come up with ways to use their natural learning strengths. Supplement their classroom learning with stories of heroes of the faith and what it means to be a man or woman of character and integrity.

You will always be your children's teacher, although your roles will change as they grow up. Each child will eventually build a life apart from your home, but the foundation you've built with them can last forever.

BITE-SIZED TRUTHS

- If the point of education is learning, the possibilities for doing that can be positively endless.

- We can't just put our children's education on autopilot and hope for the best. We have to get involved.

- When parents partner with their children, everyone can figure out how to do hard things—and become confident learners for the rest of their lives.

Conclusion

Reviewing Your Tools and Choices

TWICE IN MY LIFE, I (Cynthia) have had to undergo a deep and extensive background check for a position with a law enforcement organization. The more recent one was about ten years ago. After passing the lengthy and thorough investigation process, there was only one segment left. It was the standardized character and integrity test, 140 questions asking about my personal background—any drug use, criminal history, and so on. It was known as a written lie detector.

Having nothing to hide, I wasn't worried on the morning I showed up at the police headquarters to take the test. When I was handed the test booklet and answer sheet, though, I was taken off guard. The answer sheet had orange bubbles, not the customary green ones. I'm very visual, and I was thrown by the change in color. But after getting over the initial shock, I completed the test without any problem. Or so I thought.

A few days later, I met with the lieutenant. "I see by your test that you never finished high school," she said.

I protested. "Not only did I graduate from high school, but I even have a master's degree!"

She continued. "And it says here that you admit to having stolen quite a bit of money from a former employer."

I gasped. "*What?* That's ridiculous! That's absolutely not true."

Fortunately, they were willing to investigate what went wrong. It turns out that at the very beginning of the test, still flustered by the wrong color of the test bubbles, I got off by one line—and it altered every other answer I gave. Wow! What a vivid illustration of the fact that you cannot accurately judge a person by the results of a standardized test.

Throughout your children's school-age years, you may be tempted to focus on their achievement of grades and standardized test scores to measure their academic success. Don't give in to that.

Instead, get to know each child individually and recognize his or her unique potential. Put the concepts in this book to the test. Talk to your children about what frustrates them in their current educational setting. Ask them what would make it easier; challenge them to think about solutions. You may be surprised by how much more cooperative your children will be when they get to figure out for themselves what works.

Let me suggest a few general dos and don'ts:

- Don't expect any of your children to be just like you or your spouse. Each of you has been given unique and wonderful strengths, and working together can yield great rewards.

- Don't put your children's education on autopilot. Keep your hands on the wheel. This isn't a period of years that you just have to get through; this is the foundation for success for the rest of their lives.
- Don't relinquish their youth to those who will not teach them to honor and cherish the Creator who made them.
- Do remember to keep in mind an important question: *What's the point?* What are you trying to accomplish? How many ways are there to do it? Yours may not be the only way or even the best.
- Do deliberately teach them to recognize, appreciate, and use their natural strengths when they need to learn.
- Do everything in your power to protect your children from those who would try to instill in them a secular worldview instead of a biblical one and therefore negatively influence how they think.

Remember, parents are a child's first and most influential teachers. Where you send your children to school can either reinforce or erase much of what you've taught. Don't make the decision lightly. The path you choose may very well mean that great sacrifice is necessary. Just be sure it isn't your children who are being sacrificed.

One thing is certain: However your children are educated, you'll be amazed at how effective learning can be when you teach them *the way they learn.*

Notes

1 | PROBLEM: PUBLIC SCHOOLS ARE FAILING

1. Margaret Flavin, "Teachers Union to Parents: Educators Know Better Than Parents," *The Gateway Pundit* (blog), November 14, 2022, https://www.thegatewaypundit.com/2022/11/teachers-union-parents-educators-know-better-parents.
2. Tim Walker, "'Education Is Political': Neutrality in the Classroom Shortchanges Students," *neaToday* (National Education Association), December 11, 2018, https://www.nea.org/nea-today/all-news-articles/education-political-neutrality-classroom-shortchanges-students.
3. Tim Walker, "Education Is Political."
4. "Education Rankings by Country 2023," World Population Review, accessed August 5, 2023, https://worldpopulationreview.com/country-rankings/education-rankings-by-country.
5. Alvin Parker, "84+ Literacy Statistics in the US for 2023 (Data & Facts)," *Prosperity for All* (blog), March 15, 2023, https://prosperityforamerica.org/literacy-statistics.
6. Peter Myers, "How Black Lives Matter Is Moving into the Schools," *New York Post*, August 29, 2019, https://nypost.com/2019/08/29/how-black-lives-matter-is-moving-into-the-schools.
7. "Who We Are," Black Lives Matter at School, accessed May 20, 2023, https://www.blacklivesmatteratschool.com.
8. "13 Guiding Principles," Black Lives Matter at School, accessed May 20, 2023, https://www.blacklivesmatteratschool.com/13-guiding-principles.html.
9. "Week of Action Starter Kit," Black Lives Matter at School, accessed May 20, 2023, https://www.blacklivesmatteratschool.com/week-of-action-starter-kit.html.

10. "Who We Are," Planned Parenthood, accessed May 31, 2023, https://www
.plannedparenthood.org/about-us/who-we-are.

2 | PROBLEM: ONE-SIZE-FITS-ALL EDUCATION

1. Keri D. Ingraham, "A Case for Disrupting K-12 Education in the U.S.,"
Discovery Institute, August 23, 2022, https://www.discovery.org/education
/2022/08/23/a-case-for-disrupting-k-12-education-in-the-u-s.
2. "Students with Disabilities," National Center for Education Statistics,
accessed May 20, 2023, https://nces.ed.gov/programs/coe/indicator/cgg.
3. Thomas Armstrong, PhD, "12 Ways to Revitalize U.S. Education: If
Einstein Ran the Schools," American Institute for Learning and Human
Development, https://www.institute4learning.com/resources/articles
/if-einstein-ran-the-schools.
4. Thomas Armstrong, PhD, "12 Ways to Revitalize U.S. Education."
5. "What Is ADHD?" American Psychiatric Association, June 2022,
https://www.psychiatry.org/patients-families/adhd/what-is-adhd.
6. "The Next Era of Human-Machine Partnerships," Dell Technologies and
the Institute for the Future, 2017, https://www.delltechnologies.com/content
/dam/delltechnologies/assets/perspectives/2030/pdf/SR1940_IFTFforDell
Technologies_Human-Machine_070517_readerhigh-res.pdf.

3 | A SIMPLE FORMULA FOR SUCCESS

1. Suzie Dalien, "The History of Special Education," *Special Ed Resource*
(blog), accessed May 20, 2023, https://specialedresource.com/history
-special-education.
2. "What Are Learning Disabilities?" Learning Disabilities Association of
America, accessed August 5, 2023, https://ldaamerica.org/advocacy/lda
-position-papers/what-are-learning-disabilities.
3. "What Are Learning Disabilities?" National Institute of Neurological
Disorders and Stroke, accessed January 20, 2023, https://www.ninds
.nih.gov/health-information/disorders/learning-disabilities.

4 | WHAT HELPS YOU CONCENTRATE?

1. "School Desks and Chronic Back Pain," *Prairie Spine* (blog), Prairie Spine
and Pain Institute, September 23, 2013, https://prairiespine.com/spine-care
/school-desks-and-chronic-back-pain.
2. "How Light Impacts Psychology and Mood in Education," TCP (Technical
Consumer Products, Inc.), November 15, 2021, https://www.tcpi.com/how
-light-impacts-psychology-mood-in-education.

7 | PUTTING CHILDREN FIRST
1. Oswald Chambers, *My Utmost for His Highest Journal* (Ulrichsville, OH: Barbour Publishing, 1963), September 2 entry.

8 | WHY WOULD YOU HOMESCHOOL?
1. Carolyn Thompson, "Homeschooling surged during the pandemic. As schools reopen, many parents continue to educate their children," *Fortune*, April 14, 2022, https://fortune.com/2022/04/14/pandemic-homeschooling-surge-us-school-reopening.
2. Carolyn Thompson, "Homeschooling surged during the pandemic."
3. Michael J. Dillon, "A historic surge in homeschooling continues despite the return of in-person learning," *The Lion*, May 2, 2022, https://readlion.com/2022/05/02/a-historic-surge-in-homeschooling-continues-despite-the-return-of-in-person-learning.
4. Carolyn Thompson, "Homeschooling surged during the pandemic."
5. David French, "The Transgender Straw Broke the Camel's Back: It's Time to Declare Independence from Public Schools," *National Review*, May 13, 2016, https://www.nationalreview.com/2016/05/transgender-school-edict-public-schools-need-conservative-reform.
6. Paul Washer, AZ Quotes, accessed May 22, 2023, https://www.azquotes.com/quote/703924.
7. John Taylor Gatto, AZ Quotes, accessed May 22, 2023, https://www.azquotes.com/author/5389-John_Taylor_Gatto.

10 | SURPRISING NEW OPTIONS
1. Learn more about Connections at https://connectionsnw.org.

References and Resources

OTHER BOOKS BY CYNTHIA ULRICH TOBIAS

Tobias, Cynthia Ulrich. *Every Child Can Succeed: Making the Most of Your Child's Learning Style*. Colorado Springs: Focus on the Family.
This book is filled with practical ideas for applying learning styles to motivation, discipline, and much more. Copyright-free profiles in the appendix can help parents and children record and summarize style strengths for every teacher.

Tobias, Cynthia Ulrich. *I Hate School: How to Help Your Child Love Learning*. Grand Rapids: HarperCollins.
This book has dozens of practical strategies for helping your child succeed in school by focusing on strengths and taking charge of his or her own success. It features a special section for homeschool parents.

Tobias, Cynthia Ulrich and Sue Acuña. *Middle School: The Inside Story: What Kids Tell Us, But Don't Tell You*. Colorado Springs: Focus on the Family.
This book offers direct quotes and real-life anecdotes along with fresh insights into understanding and bringing out the best in middle schoolers (ages 10–14).

Tobias, Cynthia Ulrich. *The Way They Learn: How to Discover and Teach to Your Child's Strengths*. Colorado Springs: Focus on the Family.
An international bestseller, this entertaining and practical book should be required reading for any parents or teachers who truly want to help their children succeed. These concepts are powerful tools for bringing out the best in every child.

Tobias, Cynthia Ulrich. *The Way We Work: Taking Charge of Your Own Success.* Seattle: Apple Street.

This book gives practical advice and information for understanding how our inborn learning strengths can make a world of difference in how we understand and interact with others. It offers a powerful plan for transforming your on-the-job relationships and a valuable resource for students preparing to enter the workplace.

Tobias, Cynthia Ulrich. *You Can't Make Me (But I Can Be Persuaded): Strategies for Bringing Out the Best in Your Strong-Willed Child.* Colorado Springs: Waterbrook.

This book is packed with immediately useful strategies to drastically reduce the level of tension in the home or classroom and practical strategies for turning conflict into cooperation and building a stronger, more positive relationship with your strong-willed child without letting go of accountability or accepting excuses for bad behavior.

FOUNDATIONAL COGNITIVE STYLE RESEARCH

These are some of the earliest researchers on this topic, whose work has stood the test of time. The research is solid, empirical, and reliable. Many have presented variations on these basic principles without ever referring to the original research, but we (Cynthia and Mary Jo) believe it is a critical part of truly understanding how our minds work.

Barbe, Walter B. *Growing Up Learning: Identifying and Teaching Children with Different Learning Styles.* Washington, DC: Acropolis Books.

Although this book is currently out of print, your trip to the library to read it will be well worth your while. The former editor of *Highlights* magazine offers a wealth of information about auditory, visual, and kinesthetic modalities. You'll find age-appropriate checklists and dozens of suggestions for helping your child learn in many different ways.

Dunn, Rita, Ed.D., and Dr. Kenneth Dunn. *Teaching Students through Their Individual Learning Styles: A Practical Approach.* Reston, VA: Reston Publishing Company.

This book provides the original landmark research from St. John's University in New York that brought practical techniques and strategies to classroom teachers and expanded into doctoral degrees in learning styles.

Witkin, Herman A. "Cognitive Styles in the Educational Setting," *New York University Education Quarterly*, 1977, 14–20.

Witkin, Herman A., Carol A. Moore, Donald R. Goodenough, and Patricia W. Cox. "Field Dependent and Field-Independent Cognitive Styles and Their Educational Implications," *Review of Educational Research*. Winter 1977, Vol. 47 #1, 1–64.
These are two of the cornerstone articles by researcher Herman Witkin, laying out the foundation of his research model.

HOMESCHOOL

Resources and references are constantly changing and being updated. The best way to stay current is to keep up with your favorite sites online. Here are two recommendations.

Home School Legal Defense Association, https://hslda.org/get-started.
This should be your number one go-to site. It offers up-to-date general information about multiple aspects of homeschooling, including sections for each specific state.

Cathy Duffy Reviews, https://cathyduffyreviews.com.
Cathy Duffy has been reviewing curriculum for the homeschooling community since 1984. Her site and resources are constantly being updated.

Help your teen grow her faith in Jesus!

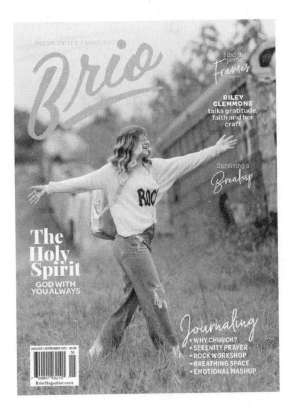

Brio delivers what your teen girl wants to read—entertainment, health, and beauty ideas—and affirms the values you've taught her. Every issue features interactive activities, faith journaling pages, and inspiring practical articles on today's issues.

BrioMagazine.com

Reclaiming Education
STUDENT WORKBOOK

A free resource for educators to use with their students
in preschool through high school and beyond.

The workbook is designed to be used together with the book

Reclaiming Education:
Teach Your Child to Be a Confident Learner

by Cynthia Ulrich Tobias with Mary Jo Dean.

GET THE WORKBOOK

Discover your own learning strengths and
share what you know with those you are teaching.

FOCUS ON THE FAMILY®